The Border Antiquities Of England And Scotland: Comprising Specimens Of Architecture And Sculpture, And Other Vestiges Of Former Ages, Accompanied By Descriptions, Volumes 1-2 - Primary Source Edition

Sir Walter Scott

Engraved by J.ᵗⁱ Greig from a Painting by L. Clennell, for the Border Antiquities of England and Scotland.

THE CHAPEL IN THE

CASTLE AT NEWCASTLE, NORTHUMBERLAND.

London, Publish'd May 1.ᵗ 1812, for the Proprietors by Longman, & C.º Paternoster Row.

Engraved by J. Smith, from a Painting by L. Clennell for the Border Antiquities of England and Scotland.

West ENTRANCE to
HOLYROOD CHAPEL
Edinburgh.

THE

BORDER ANTIQUITIES

OF

ENGLAND AND SCOTLAND;

COMPRISING

SPECIMENS OF ARCHITECTURE AND SCULPTURE.

AND OTHER VESTIGES OF FORMER AGES,

ACCOMPANIED BY DESCRIPTIONS.

TOGETHER WITH

ILLUSTRATIONS OF REMARKABLE INCIDENTS IN BORDER HISTORY AND TRADITION, AND ORIGINAL POETRY.

BY WALTER SCOTT, ESQ.

VOL. I.

LONDON:

PRINTED FOR LONGMAN, HURST, REES, ORME, AND BROWN, PATERNOSTER-ROW;
J. MURRAY, ALBEMARLE-STREET; JOHN GREIG, UPPER-STREET, ISLINGTON;
AND CONSTABLE AND CO. EDINBURGH.

1814.

BORDER ANTIQUITIES.

Horrida præcipue cui gens, assuetaque multo
Venatu nemorum, duris Æquicula glebis :
Armati terram exercent, semperque recentis
Convectare juvat prædas, et vivere rapto.

Æneid. Lib. vii. 1. 746.

a

INTRODUCTION.

———————

THE frontier regions of most great kingdoms, while they retain that character, are unavoidably deficient in subjects for the antiquary. The ravages to which they are exposed, and the life to which the inhabitants are condemned by circumstances, are equally unfavourable to the preservation of the monuments of antiquity. Even in military antiquities such countries, though the constant scene of war, do not usually abound. The reason is obvious. The same circumstances of alarm and risque require occupation of the same points of defence; and, as the modes of attack and of fortification change, the ancient bulwarks of cities and castles are destroyed, in order to substitute newer and more approved modes of defence. The case becomes different, however, when, losing by conquest or by union their character as a frontier, scenes once the theatre of constant battle, inroad, defence, and retaliation, have been for two hundred years converted into the abode of peace and tranquillity. Numerous castles left to moulder in massive ruins; fields where the memory of ancient battles still lives among the descendants of those by whom they were fought or witnessed ; the very line of demarcation, which, separating the two countries, though no longer hostile, induces the inhabitants of each to cherish their separate traditions,—unite to render these regions interesting to the topographical historian or antiquary. This is peculiarly the case on the border of Scotland and England. The recollection of their former hostility has much of interest and nothing of enmity. The evidences of its existence bear, at the same time, witness to the remoteness of its date ; and he who traverses these peaceful glens and hills to find traces of strife, must necessarily refer his researches to a period of considerable antiquity. But it was not always thus; for, since the earliest period of which we have any distinct information until the union of the crowns, the northern provinces of England, and the southern counties of Scotland, have been the scenes of inveterate hostilities, commenced and maintained with fury, even before the names of Scotland and England were acknowledged by history.

Our earliest authentic acquaintance with these transactions is during the Roman period of English history, and commences with the invasion of Agricola, whose efforts carried his invading arms almost 81. to the extremity of Caledonia. At this period the Border counties of England and Scotland were inhabited by three nations. Those Britons lying to the east, and possessing one-half of Northumberland, and extending from the northern bank of the South Tyne to the Frith of Forth, were called the Ottadini. Westward of this powerful nation lay the Gadeni, who held the west part of Northumberland, great part of Roxburghshire, Selkirk and Peebles shires, and extended also to the banks of the Forth, embracing West-Lothian. This country being mountainous, and remaining forest-ground to a late period, the Gadeni were probably a less populous nation than the inhabitants of the more fertile country to the east. Westward of the Gadeni, and extending to the sea-coast of the Atlantic, lay the Selgovæ, having the Solway Frith for their southern limit. These nations Agricola found each occupying a strong country, and animated with the courage necessary to defend it. But their arms and discipline were unable to resist those of the Romans. A brief statement of their means of defence at this remote period naturally commences the Introduction to the Border Antiquities.

The towns of the ancient Britons were fortified in the ordinary manner of barbarians, with ditches, single or double, occupying the angles of the eminences, which were naturally selected for their site, and being, of course, irregular in their form. The earth was thrown up so as to form a steep *glacis* to the outside, and was sometimes faced with stones, in order to add to its height, and increase the acclivity; this formed the rampart of the place, and the gates, generally two or three in number, were placed where access was most convenient. One of the most perfect of these forts is situated in the neighbourhood of the celebrated Catrail, a work of antiquity to be afterwards briefly noticed, just where that limitary fence crosses the farm of Rink, belonging to Mr. Pringle of Fairnilee. The fort occupies the crest of an eminence near the junction of the rivers Tweed and Ettricke, which has an extensive prospect in every direction; and, though in the neighbourhood of higher hills, is too distant to be itself commanded by them in a military sense. There are two ramparts, the first of earth and loose stones, but the interior consisting of immense blocks of stone, disposed so as to form a rude wall, and faced with earth and turf within. The permanence of these massive materials seems to have insured that of the building, for they defy all ordinary efforts of the agriculturist, too apt to consider such works as cumberers of the ground. The fortress has too gates, one to the east and the other to the west, with something like traverses for protecting and defending the approach. This remarkable fortress is surrounded by others of less consequence, serving as out-posts, and has plainly been a hill-fort of great importance belonging to the Gadeni. It is, probably, more ancient than the Catrail itself.

There are not to be found, on the Border, any of those vitrified appearances which are to be found in Craig Phactraig, and other Highland fortifications, and which seem to intimate that fire was used in building or in destroying them. We may therefore conclude, that the stones employed in constructing them were less fusible than those found in the shires of Forfar, Kincardine, and Aberdeen.

If we can trust a popular tradition, the singular ancient structures called Peghts, or Picts Houses, common in the Highlands, Western Isles, and Orcades, were also to be found in the Border. The inhabitants point out small rings, or elevated circles, where these *Duns*, as they are called, are said to have stood. In Liddesdale, particularly, more than one of these are shown. But whether, like those of Dun-Dornadilla in Sutherland, and Mousa in Shetland, they were built of stones arranged in the form of a glass-house, and containing a series of concentric galleries within the thickness of the wall, must be left to conjecture. Mr. Chalmers seems to have considered them as common hill-forts.

These fortresses, so constructed, the natives defended with javelins and bows and arrows, the usual weapons of savages. The arrow-heads, made of flint, are frequently found, and are called, by the vulgar, elf-arrow-heads, from being, as they supposed, formed by the fairies or elves. At a later period, the Britons used copper and brass heads for arrows, javelins, and spears, which are found of various sizes and shapes near their habitations. In like manner, from the specimens found on the Borders, there appears to have been a gradual improvement in the construction of battle-axes and weapons of close fight. The original Celts, or axes, are of polished stone, shaped something like a wedge. These are found of all sizes, some seeming intended for felling trees, and others for warlike purposes ; and others again so very small, that they could only be designed for carving or dividing food.* When, however, this degree of refinement was attained, it was obvious that some improvement in the material of which the implements were formed, could not be far distant.

Accordingly, brass Celts, or battle-axes, seem to have been the next step in advance ; and these are of various forms, more or less rude, as the knowledge of the art of working in metals began to advance. The first and most rude form of the brass Celt, usually found in the urns under sepulchral cairns, is a sort of brazen wedge, having an edge, however, rounded like that of an axe, about three inches

---

* These are certainly Celtic weapons ; yet they cannot be considered as peculiar to that people. They have been found in considerable numbers in the Shetland Isles, which were evidently first settled by the Scandinavians. The natives suppose them to be thunderbolts, and account the possession of one of them a charm. Mr. Collector Ross of Lerwick presented the author of this Introduction with six of these weapons found in Shetland. It is said the stone of which they are constructed cannot be found in these islands. The natives preserve them, from a superstitious idea that they are *thunderbolts,* and preserve houses against the effects of lightning.

broad in the face. The shape of these weapons points out the probable mode of attaching them to handles, by hollowing out the sides, and leaving deep ledges; so that, if we conceive the abrupt angle at the root of an oak branch to have been divided by fire, the axe might have been inserted between the remaining pieces; and the whole being lashed fast by a thong, for securing which provision is often, though not uniformly, made by a loop in the brazen head, a battle-axe of formidable weight and edge was immediately obtained. The next step of improvement was that of casting the axe hollow instead of solid, so that the crooked part of the handle being inserted into the concave part of the axe as into a sheath, a far more solid and effectual weapon was obtained, and at less expence of metal, than when the handle was weakened by burning, and divided into two portions, which overlapped, as it were, the solid axe. It seems probable that the provincial Britons learned this improvement from their masters, for the hollow axes resemble those of the Romans in shape and size, and are sometimes decorated round the rim where they join the handle, with a rude attempt at moulding. But the hollow axe was, like the more rude solid implement, secured to the handle by thongs, as the loop or fixed ring left for the purpose usually testifies.

The next step taken by the Britons, in improving their warlike weapons, seems to have been the fastening the metal with which they were shod to the wooden handles, by means of broad-headed copper or brass nails, secured by similar heads on the opposite side, and thus effectually rivetted to the wood. This seems to have been the mode of shafting a weapon, like a very broad-headed javelin or spear, found near Friarshaugh, opposite to Melrose, the seat of

John Tod, Esq.* This curious weapon is about a palm's-breadth at the bottom, tapering to the length of about nine inches, or perhaps more, (for it is considerably decayed towards the point) dimensions greatly exceeding those of the Roman *pilum*, or javelin. It resembles pretty much those weapons which the Californian Indians manufacture out of copper, and secure, by broad-headed copper nails, to handles made of bone. These are now used by the Californians as they were probably employed by the Gadeni, or northern Britons in general, to complete and secure the union of the wooden shaft and metal head.

Short brazen swords of a peculiar shape are also occasionally, though rarely, found in these districts; they are uniformly formed narrow towards the handle, broad about the middle of the blade, and again tapering to a point at the extremity. Such weapons, by the common consent of antiquaries, have hitherto been termed Roman swords. They are, however, unlike in shape to those usually represented on Roman monuments, which are almost uniformly of an equal breadth from the handle, until they taper, or rather slope off suddenly, to form a sharp and double-edged point. The metal employed may also lead us to doubt the general opinion which gives these weapons to the Romans. That the arts of Rome under the emperors, and for a length of time before, had attained to working steel, a metal so much superior to brass for the formation of military weapons, and its general use in manufacturing arms, is suffici-

---

* Presented to the author by Mr. Tod. Notwithstanding what is said in the text, it may, perhaps, be thought a specimen of the Roman Pilum, though differing in the size and mode of shafting.

ently testified by their employing the word *ferrum*, to signify battle
in general. It may, no doubt, be urged, that in size and shortness
the brass swords in question differ from the long blades generally
used by barbarians. But, without stopping to consider the variety
of weapon which might exist in different tribes; without dwelling on
the awkward and useless increasing breadth and thickness of the
blades in the middle, which look very like the first gradation from a
club to a sword; without even founding upon the probability that,
after the Roman discipline had become known to the barbarians by
fatal experience, they had tried (and certainly they had time enough
to have done so) to make a rude imitation of the Roman sword in the
metal which was most easily manufactured,—without resting upon
any of these things, we may require the evidence that the Romans
ever, within the period of their recorded history, used brazen swords.
That the Greeks did so in the remote days of Homer cannot be
doubted, and certainly from the same reason that we ascribe these
weapons to the Britons, namely, that to fuse brass is a more easy and
obvious manufacture than to work steel. But that the Romans ever
employed swords of this inferior metal during the period of their
history which is recorded, we have no warrant to believe. Virgil,
an antiquary and a scholar, as well as a poet, in describing the various
tribes of Italy, who assembled under Turnus, does indeed mention
one nation whose warriors wore swords of brass—

> Et quos maliferæ despectant mænia Abellæ
> Teutonico ritu soliti torquere cateias ;
> Tegmina quîs capitum raptus de subere cortex ;
> Eratæque micant peltæ, micat æreus ensis.
>
> ÆNEID. Lib. VII.

On this passage there are three things to be observed. First, that this mountain and rude tribe is described as retaining the ancient customs of the Teutones. Secondly, that the rest of their armour and weapons, as the helmets made of cork, and the Gallic sling, or harpoon called *catela*, are given along with the brazen narrow buckler, or *pelta*, and the brazen sword in question, as marks of a rude tribe, unprovided with such weapons as the other Italians used at the supposed arrival of Æneas. Besides, swords of this description have been found in the western islands, or Hebrides, to which the Romans never penetrated; and they have also been found in Ireland. Nay, we are assured, that, in one instance, not only the sword-blades, but the mould for casting weapons of that description, have been found in the kingdom last mentioned,—facts which certainly go far to establish that these brazen swords, which in breadth and thickness have a spherical form, are of British, not of Roman manufacture.

The battle array of the British in these northern districts, mountainous and woody, and full of morasses, must have been chiefly on foot. But we are assured by Tacitus that they, as well as the Southern Britons, used the chariot of war. All the Celtic chiefs seem to have gloried in being car-borne, and are so described by the Welsh, the Irish, and the Gaelic bards. It is probable that men of distinction alone used this distinguished, but inconvenient, mode of fighting; and that as the cavalry of the Romans formed a separate rank in the state, so the *covinarii* in the northern parts of Britain consisted of the chiefs and their distinguished followers only. Indeed the difficulty which such squadrons must have found in acting, unless upon Salisbury plain, or ground equally level, must have rendered the use of them in the north rather a point of imposing splendour than of real advantage. The charioteers of the Caledonians do indeed seem to have made a considerable part of their force in the memorable battle which Agricola fought against Galgacus near the foot of the Grampian Hills. But we are to consider, that at this important period, common danger had driven the chiefs to form a general league, so that every sort of force which they could draw together appeared in its utmost proportion; and those war-chariots, assembled from all quarters, augmented by those also of the Southern Britons who had retired before the conqueror to these last recesses of freedom, bore, probably, an unusual proportion to the extent of their forces. That they fought valiantly, the Romans themselves admit; and they certainly possessed the mode of managing that very awkward engine called a chariot-of-war, where even the lower grounds are unequal and broken by ravines and morasses, with as much, or more effect than the Persians, of a more ancient date, upon their extensive and level plains. There is, as far as we know, but one representation of a chariot of this period existing in Scotland. It occurs in the church-yard of Meigle, in a neighbourhood famous for possessing the earliest sculptural monuments respecting the events of antiquity. The chariot is drawn by a single horse, and carries two persons besides the driver.* Chariots used in war are the invention of a rude age, before men adventured to break horses for riding. In a rough country, like Scotland, they could be but rarely employed with advantage, and must soon have fallen into disuse.

Of the worship of the Northern Britons we have no distinct traces;

---

* See an engraving in Pennant's Tour, vol. III.

but we cannot doubt that it was Druidical. The circles of detached stones, supposed to be proper to that mode of worship, abound in various places on the Border; and, although there may be good reason to doubt whether the presence of those monuments is in all other cases to be positively referred to the worship of the Druids,* yet there is no reason to think that the religion of the Ottadini, Gadeni, or Selgovæ, differed from that of the southern British tribes. We know, at least, one instance of the Druid's Adder-stone, a glass bead so termed, being found on the Borders. This curious relique is now in possession of a lady in Edinburgh. They appear, however, to have worshipped some local deities, whom the urbanity of Roman paganism acknowledged and adopted with the usual deference to the religion of the conquered. In the station of Habitancum, now called Risingham, near the village of Woodburn in Redesdale, was found a Roman altar dedicated to Mogon, a god of the Gadeni; and there is one in the Advocates' Library of Edinburgh inscribed to the *Divi Campestres*, or Fairies. It was found in the romantic vicinity of Roxburgh Castle.

---

* The most stately monument of this sort in Scotland, and probably inferior to none in England, excepting Stone-henge, is formed by what are called the Standing Stones of Stenhouse, in the island of Pomona in the Orknies, where it can scarcely be supposed that Druids ever penetrated; at least, it is certain, that the common people now consider it as a Scandinavian monument; and, according to an ancient custom, a couple who are desirous to attach themselves by more than an ordinary vow of fidelity, join hands through the round hole which is in one of the stones. This they call the promise of Odin. The Ting-walls, or places where the Scandinavians held their comitia, were surrounded by circles of stones as well as the places of Druid worship; and instances of this occur even in Norway. But, indeed, the general idea of setting up a circle of stones to mark the space allotted for the priests, or nobles, while the vulgar remained without its precincts, seems likely to be common to many early nations.

The funeral monuments of the Celtic tribes on the Border are numerous, and consist of the cairns, or heaps of stones, so frequently piled on remarkable spots. On opening them, there is usually found in the centre a small square inclosure of stones set on edge, with bones, and arms such as we have already described. There is frequently found within this stone-chest, or *cist-vaen*, as it is called by the Welch, an urn filled with ashes and small beads made of coal. The manufacture of these urns themselves is singular. The skill of the artist appears not to have been such as to enable him to form his urn completely before subjecting it to the operation of the fire. He therefore appears to have first shaped the rude vessel of the dimensions which he desired, and then baked· it into potter's-ware. On the vessel thus formed and hardened, he afterwards seems to have spread a very thin coat of unbaked clay, on which he executed his intended ornaments, and which was left to harden at leisure. The scrolls and mouldings thus hatched on the outside of these urns are not always void of taste. In these tombs and elsewhere have been repeatedly found the *Eudorchawg*, the *Torques*, or chain, formed of twisted gold, worn by the Celtic chiefs of rank. In the fatal battle of Cattraeth, in which the Celtic tribes of the middle marches sustained a decisive defeat from the Saxons who occupied Northumberland, Berwickshire, and Lothian, somewhere, probably, about the junction of Tweed and Ettrick, and in the neighbourhood of the Catrail, there fell three hundred chieftains, all of whom, as appears from the elegy of Aneurin, a sad survivor of the slaughter, wore the Torques of gold. It is not a chain forged into rings, but is formed of thin rods of flexible gold twisted into loops which pass through each other, and form oblong links. This ornament appears

to have been common to the chiefs of all Celtic tribes ; and undoubtedly Manlius had his surname of Torquatus from killing a Gallic chief
so decorated.   The broach for securing the mantle has been repeatedly found in the Borders.   It is also an ancient Celtic ornament.

The Druids are understood to have had no use of coins ; yet it is
singular, that, on a place near to Cainmore in Tweeddale, there
were found, along with a fine specimen of the *Eudorchawg*, a number of round drops of gold of different sizes, greatly resembling the
coins of the native Hindhus, and of which it is difficult to make any
thing unless we suppose them intended to circulate as specie.   May
it not be conjectured, that the provincial Britons fell on this expedient
of maintaining a circulating medium of commerce, from the example
of the Romans ?

In the Lochermoss, near Dumfries, have been found canoes made
out of a single trunk like those of Indians, which served the aboriginal
inhabitants for the purposes of fishing.   But in the time of the Romans, the Britons had acquired the art of making light barks, called
Curraghs, covered with hides like the boats of the Esquimaux.   This
brief account of the hill-forts, sepulchres, arms, religion, and means of
embarkment, possessed by the three Celtic tribes whom the Romans
found in possession of the Borders, completes a brief and general view
of the British antiquities of the district.

The ROMAN Antiquities found in these districts are of such number and importance as might be expected from the history of their
northern warfare, and the policy which they adopted to preserve
their conquests.   Even the ambition of a Roman conqueror, to extend, as far as possible, the limits of the empire, could not blind the
successors of Agricola to the inconveniences which would be in-

curred in attempting a total conquest of Britain. That the invaders would defeat the natives as often as they might be imprudent enough to hazard a general action, was highly probable; but to win an engagement, or overrun a succession of mountains, lakes, towns, and morasses, was more easy than to establish and maintain amongst them the necessary garrisons and military points of communication, without which, the soldiers whom the victor might leave to maintain his conquests, must unquestionably have fallen victims to famine and the attacks of the barbarians. The Romans, therefore, renouncing the enticing but fallacious idea of maintaining a military occupation of the Caledonian mountains, set themselves seriously to protect such part of the island as was worth keeping and capable of being rendered secure. It may be much doubted, whether they paid even to the southern parts of Scotland the compliment of supposing them a desirable conquest. But to intersect them by roads, and occupy them with camps and garrisons, was necessary for the protection of the more valuable country of England.*

Accordingly, the earliest measure taken for the protection of the Roman province in Britain, was the original wall of Hadrian, extending from the Frith of Solway to the mouth of the Tyne. Within this line the country was accounted civilized, and what was retained beyond it, was strongly occupied and secured by fortresses. At a later period, Lollius Urbicus, during the reign of Antoninus, formed a similar wall greatly in advance of the first, between the

---

* The learned author of Caledonia concludes, that these roads were extended even to the north of Aberdeenshire. It is impossible to mention this work without acknowledging with gratitude the brilliant light it has cast on many parts of Scottish history hitherto so imperfectly understood.

Friths, namely, of Forth and Clyde.   It was a rampart of earth, with A.D. 139.
a deep ditch, military road, and forts, or stations, from point to
point, but appears to have proved insufficient to curb the incursions
of the tribes without the province, or to prevent the insurrection of
those within its precints.   The Emperor Severus found the country
betwixt the walls of Hadrian and that erected by Lollius Urbicus,
during the reign of Antoninus, in such a state of disorder, that, after
an expedition in order to intimidate rather than to subdue the more
northern tribes, he appears to have fixed upon the more southern
barrier as that which was capable of being effectually maintained and
defended ; and, although it is not to be presumed that he formally
renounced the sovereignty of the space between the Friths of Solway and of the Forth and the Clyde, yet it is probable he only
retained military possession of the most tenable stations, resting the
ultimate defence of the province upon the wall of Hadrian, which he
rebuilt with stone, and fortified with great care.   Betwixt the years
211, being the æra of the death of Severus, and 409, the date of the
final abandonment of Britain by the Romans, the space between the
two walls, entitled by the Romans the province of Valentia, was the
scene of constant conflict, insurrection, and incursion ; and towards
the latter part of this tumultuous period the exterior line of Antoninus was totally abandoned, and the southern wall itself was found
as insufficient as that of Antoninus to curb the increasing audacity of
the free tribes.

From this brief deduction it may be readily conjectured, that the
Roman Antiquities found in the districts to which this introduction
relates, must be chiefly of a military nature.   We find, accordingly,
neither theatres, baths, nor temples, such as have been discovered

in Southern Britain, but military roads, forts, castles, and camps, in great abundance.

The principal Roman curiosity which the Border presents, is certainly the wall of Severus, with the various strong stations connected with it. The execution of all these military works bears the stamp of the Roman tool, which aimed at labouring for ages. The most remarkable is the wall itself, a work constructed with the greatest solidity and strength. The ravages continually made upon it for fourteen centuries, when any one in the neighbourhood found use for the well-cut stones of which it is built, have not been able to obliterate the traces of this bulwark of the empire. The wall was twelve feet high, guarded by flanking towers and exploratory turrets, and eight feet broad, running over precipices and through morasses. The facing on both sides was of square freestone, the interior of rubble run in with quicklime between the two faces, and uniting the whole in a solid mass. The earthen rampart of Hadrian lies to the north of it, and might, in many places, be used as a first line of defence. It is not clear in what manner the Roman troops sallied from this line of defence when circumstances rendered it necessary. No gates appear, except at the several stations. A paved military way may be traced parallel to the walls, in most places, for the purpose of sending reinforcements from one point to another. No less than eighteen *stations*, or fortresses, of importance, have been traced on the line of the wall. The most entire part of this celebrated monument, which is now, owing to the progress of improvement and enclosure, subjected to constant dilapidation, is to be found at a place called Glenwhelt, in the neighbourhood of Gilsland Spaw.❋

❋ Its height may be guessed, from the following characteristic anecdote of the late Mr.

The number of forts and stations extending along the wall from west to east, some in front to receive the first attack of the enemy, some behind the wall to serve as rallying places, or to accommodate the troops destined to maintain the defence, render this magnificent undertaking upon the whole one of the most remarkable monuments of history. It differs from the Great Wall of China, to which it has been compared, as much as a work fortified with military skill, and having various gradations and points of defence supporting each other, is distinct from the simple idea of a plain curtain or wall. It was not until the hearts of the defenders had entirely failed them, that the barbarous tribes of the north burst over this rampire.

With the same regard to posterity which dignified all their undertakings, the Romans were careful to transmit to us, by inscriptions still extant, the time at which these works were carried on, and the various cohorts and legions by whom different parts were executed. These, with altars and pieces of sculpture, have been every where dug up in the vicinity of the wall, and form a most valuable department of Border Antiquities, though not entering into the scope of the following work.

Joseph Ritson, whose zeal for accuracy was so marked a feature in his investigations. That eminent antiquary, upon an excursion to Scotland, favoured the author with a visit. The wall was mentioned; and Mr. Ritson, who had been misinformed by some ignorant person at Hexham, was disposed strongly to dispute that any reliques of it yet remained. The author mentioned the place in the text, and said there was as much of it standing as would break the neck of Mr. Ritson's informer were he to fall from it. Of this careless and metaphorical expression Mr. Ritson failed not to make a memorandum, and afterwards wrote to the author, that he had visited the place with the express purpose of jumping down from the wall in order to confute what he supposed a hyperbole. But he added, that, though not yet satisfied that it was quite high enough to break a man's neck, it was of elevation sufficient to render the experiment very dangerous.

In advancing beyond the wall, the antiquary is struck by the extreme pains bestowed by the Romans to ensure military possession of the province of Valentia. No generals before or since their time appear to have better understood the necessity of maintaining communications. A camp, or station, of importance, is usually surrounded by smaller forts at the distance of two or three miles, and, in many cases, the communication is kept up, not only by the Iters, or military roads, which traverse the country in the direction of these fortresses, but by strong lines of communication with deep ditches and rampires. Of this there are some curious and complicated remains near Melrose, where a large triangular space lying betwixt the remarkable station on Eildon Hills and those of Castlesteads and of Caldshiels, is enclosed by ditches and ramparts of great depth. There appears to have been more than one British fortress within the same space, particularly one called the Roundabout, upon a glen termed Haxlecleuch, and another very near it upon the march between the properties of Kippilaw and Abbotsford. Besides these lines of communication, there is a military road which may be distinctly traced to the Tweed, which it appears to have crossed above Newharthaugh.* It is impossible, while tracing these gigantic labours, to refrain from admiring, on the one hand, the pains and skill which is bestowed in constructing them, and, on the other, the extra-

---

* Mr. Chalmers, whose opinion is always to be mentioned with the utmost respect, seems inclined to think, that these entrenchments are the works of the provincial Britons, executed to protect them from the Saxons of Bernicia. Some bronze vessels and Roman antiquities, found by the author in improving that part of his property through which these lines run, warrant a different conclusion.

vagant ambition which stimulated the conquerors of the world to bestow so much pains for the preservation of so rude a country.

The frequent accompaniment of these camps is a Roman *tumulus* or artificial mount, for depositing the remains of their dead, of which there is a very fine specimen on the south side of the Tweed, opposite to Sir Henry Hay Macdougal's beautiful mansion of Makerston. This *tumulus* appears to have belonged to the neighbouring camp on Fairnington Moor. In these specimens of Roman pottery have been found, probably lachrymatories and the vessels sacred to the *manes*, or souls, of the deceased. These mounts might also be used for exploratory purposes.

Around the stations have, in most instances, been found Roman coins, of all reliques the most decisive, brazen axes, usually termed Roman, though perhaps not correctly to be regarded as such, and querns, or hand-mills, for grinding corn, made of two corresponding stones. Camp-kettles of bronze of various sizes are also found on the line of these roads, particularly where marshes have been drained for marl. It may, in general, be remarked, that, in Scotland, the decay of a natural forest is the generation of a bog, which accounts for so many antiquities being found by draining. Sacrificial vessels are also frequently discovered, particularly those with three feet, a handle, and a spout, which greatly resemble an old-fashioned coffeepot without its lid. Out of the entrenchment above-mentioned, connecting the fort of Castlesteads with that on Eildon Hills, was dug a pair of forceps of iron, much resembling smiths' tongs. Inscriptions have rarely been found to the north of the wall.

Such are the evidences which still remind the antiquary, that these twelve districts once formed the fence and extreme boundary of the Roman power in Britain.

No reader requires to be reminded of the scenes of desolation which followed the abdication of the Romans. All exterior defences which the wall and the forts connected with it had hitherto afforded, were broken down and destroyed, while the Picts and Scots carried on the most wasteful incursions into the flourishing provinces of the south. But the learned and indefatigable Chalmers has plainly shewed, that the tribes inheriting the late Roman province of Valentia were not subjugated by either of these more northern nations, but maintained a separate and precarious independence. These tribes, the reader will remember, were the Ottadini, Gadeni, and Selgovæ, to which were united, the Novantes of Galloway, and the Damnij of Clydesdale, who, like their Border neighbours, were inclosed between the two walls. It is probable that, according to the ancient British custom, they were governed by their separate chiefs, forming a sort of federal republic, whose array, in case of war, was subjected to the command of a dictator, termed the Pendragon. They did not long enjoy the full extent of their territory ; for, as in other parts of England, so on her northern frontiers, the invasion of the Saxons drove from their native seats the original inhabitants. It was not, however, until the year 547, that Ida, at the head of a numerous army of Anglo-Saxons, invaded and possessed himself of the greater part of Northumberland. These conquerors spread themselves on all sides, and became divided into two provinces, Deira and Bernicia. The Deirians occupied the northern division of Northumberland, with the bishopric of Durham, and made constant war with the British inhabitants of Westmoreland and Cumberland. The Saxons of Bernicia pushed their conquests northwards, possessed themselves of the ancient seats of the Ottadini and Gadeni, or the modern Berwickshire and

lower part of Roxburghshire, seized on Lothian, were probably the
first founders of Edinburgh, and warred fiercely with the natives now
cooped up in the hilly country to the westward, as also with the
Picts, who lay to the northward of these invaders. It seems highly
probable that to this people we owe the Scoto-Saxon language of the
Lowlands.* Their country is sometimes called Saxonia by ancient
writers, being the Saxon part of Scotland. The line of demarcation
which then was the subject of dispute between the Saxons and Britons, extended north and south instead of east and west, like that
which afterwards divided Scotland from England. All good antiquaries allow, that the remarkable trench called the Catrail, which
extends nearly fifty miles in the former direction, and may be traced
from near the junction of the Gala and the Tweed to the mountains of Cumberland, was intended to protect the native inhabitants
of Strath Clwyde, for thus the remaining possessions of the Ro-
manized Britons were entitled, from the too powerful Saxon invaders.
It was natural that these provincial Britons should endeavour to
make use of the same means of defence of which they had an example in the Prætentura of Antoninus, and the more elaborate wall of
Severus. The imperfect execution of the Catrail plainly shows their
inferiority of skill, while its length, and the degree of labour bestowed in the excavation, indicate their sense of its importance. This
rampart is the most curious remnant of antiquity which can be dis-

* The author has no hesitation to own that a film has fallen from his eyes on reading
the Caledonia with attention. The Picts, as conjectured by Tacitus, might have been
intermingled with settlers from Germany. But it seems probable that such emigrants
merged in the main body of the Celtic tribes just as the Scandinavians did, who, at a
later period, settled in the Hebrides and in Sutherland.

tinctly traced to this distracted period. It is a ditch and rampart of irregular dimensions, but in breadth generally from twenty to twenty-four feet, supported by many hill-forts and corresponding entrenchments, indicating the whole to have been the work of a people possessing some remnants of that military skill of which the Romans had set the example. From what Mr. Chalmers mentions of the course of Herrit's Dike, in Berwickshire, we may conjecture it to have been either a continuation of the Catrail, or a more early work of the same kind. Supposing the latter to be the case, it would seem that, when expelled from Lauderdale, the Britons fell back to the Catrail, as the Romans had done from the wall of Antoninus to that of Severus. The Catrail is very happily situated for the protection of the mountainous country, as it just commences where the valley of the Tweed becomes narrow and difficult of access, and skirts the mountains, as it runs southward. Contrary to other defences of the same sort, it was erected to save the mountaineers from the continued inroads of the inhabitants of the plains, whereas fortifications have generally been erected in the plains for precisely the opposite purpose.

It is remarkable, that the obscure contests of the Britons and Saxons yet survive in traditional song. For this we have to thank the institution of the Bards, the second rank to the Druids, and partaking of their sacred character. This order survived the fall of Druidism, and continued to perpetuate, while they exaggerated, the praise of the British chieftains who continued to fight in defence of the Cumbrian kingdom of Reged, and the more northern district of Strathclwyde. The chief of these bards, of whom we still possess the lays in the ancient British language, are Taliessin, Merlin of Caledonia, Aneurin, and Llywarch Hen. The two last appear to have been princes, and, contrary to the original rules of their order, they, as well as Merlin, were warriors.

Urien of Reged, and his son Owen, both afford high matter for the songs of the bards; and it is to the Welsh poetry also that Arthur owes a commemoration, which with the help of Geoffrey of Monmouth, was so extravagantly exaggerated by after-minstrels. These native princes, however, do certainly appear to have maintained a long struggle with the Saxons, which was frequently successful, and might have been eventually so, had not the remains of the provincial Britons been divided into two petty kingdoms of Cumbria and Strath-Clwyde, and those tribes of warriors distracted by frequent disunion among themselves. As it was, they finally lost their independence. The last king of the Cumbrian Britons, called Dunmail, was slain in battle near Ambleside, on the lake of Winandermere, where a huge cairn, raised to his memory, is still called Dunmail-Raise, and his kingdom was ceded to Scotland by the conqueror Edward in 945. Strath-Clwyde, sometimes resisting, sometimes submitting, maintained a precarious independence until about 975, when Dunwallon, the last independent king of the Northern Britons, was defeated by Kenneth III. King of the Scots, and is said to have retired to the cloister.

But although the kingdoms of Reged and Strath-Clwyde were thus melted down into the general mass of Scottish subjects, yet the British inhabitants of Valentia continued long distinguishable by their peculiar manners, customs, and laws. When Edward I. was desirous to secure his usurpation of the Scottish crown by introducing the feudal system in its full extent, and thus assimilating the laws of Eng-

d

land and Scotland, he declares, that the " customs of the Scots and the Bretts shall for the future be prohibited, and no longer practised ;" and that the king's lieutenant should submit to an assembly of the Scottish nation " the statutes made by David King of Scots, and the amendments made by other kings."   It was probably at this time that the law-treatise, entitled, *Regium Majestatem*, was compiled, with the artful design of palming upon the Scottish parliament, under the pretence of reviving their ancient jurisprudence, a system as nearly as possible resembling that of England.   Now it is proved that, until a late period, that part of modern Scotland which lay to the south of the river Forth, and bordered on the east with the Saxon province of Lothian, or Loden, was still called Britain.   Accordingly, Fordun terms Stirling a castle situated in Scotland on the confines of Britain, and says that the seal of the town of Stirling bore this legend,

Continet hoc in se pontem castrum Strivilense
Hic armis Bruti hic stant Scoti cruce tuti.

As the names of Britain and Scotland were thus preserved, the customs alluded to by Edward as proper to be abolished were those which the Scots and Britons, both nations of Celtic original, had transmitted to their descendants, and which, from the spirit of independence which they breathed, were naturally hostile to the Conqueror.   It is probable that the clan-customs and regulations were amongst those alluded to by Edward's prohibition ; at least, we shall presently see that they were the subject of jealousy to future legislators.

While the Northern Britons were maintaining the dubious and sanguinary resistance against the Saxons which we have briefly noticed, the invaders themselves were disturbed in their operations of conquest by the arrival of fresh hordes from Scandinavia, whose inroads were as distressing to the Saxon inhabitants of Northumberland and Lothian as those of their ancestors had been to the British Ottadini, whom they had expelled from those fertile provinces. The celebrated Regnar Lodbrog, renowned in the song of Scalds, led the first attack by the Danes on Northumberland. He fell; but his death was promptly and dreadfully avenged by the fresh invasion headed by his sons, Inguar and Hubba. They appear totally to have A.D.876. subverted the Saxon kingdom of Northumberland founded by Ida, and to have conquered the country as far south as York, and penetrated westward as far as Stanemore, where their invasion added to the distressed condition of the Cumbrian Britons. Aided by frequent descents of their roving countrymen, they wasted and they warred in these northern regions; and though they nominally acknowledged the royalty of Edward the Elder, the Northumbrian Danes could hardly be termed subjects of a Saxon monarch, until they were defeated by Athelstane, in the bloody and decisive battle of Brunnanburgh. The wild convulsions of the period sometimes occasioned a temporary disunion, even after this engagement; but such incidents may be regarded rather as insurrections than as a re-establishment of Northumbrian independence.

It is natural to enquire what traces still remain of the Danish invaders? The circular camps found in many places of Northumberland, and on the borders of Cumberland, are plausibly ascribed to them, and the names of their deities have been imposed upon several tracts in the same district. But we find none of those Runic monuments so common in their own country, either because they never possessed tranquillity sufficient to aim at establishing such records,

er that they were destroyed in after-ages out of hatred to the
Danish name. The taste of the Scalds, however, is to be traced in
the early English poetry which was first cultivated in the North of
England. The northern minstrels could derive no lessons from the
bards who spoke the Celtic language; their earliest attempts at poetry
were, therefore, formed on alliteration; and as late as the time of
Chaucer it was considered as the mark of a northern man to "affect
the letter."* Further of the Danes, antiquaries can trace but little.
Their independent sovereignty in Northumberland was as brief as it
was bloody; and their descendants, mixing with Saxons, and what
few might remain of the Southern Ottadini, formed the mixed race
from which, enriched by the blood of many a Norman baron, the
present Northumbrians are descended.

In the tenth century, the frontiers of England and Scotland, which
had now begun to assume these distinctive appellations, differed
greatly from the relations they bore to each other in subsequent ages.
The district of the Ottadini, conquered first by the Saxons, and afterwards by the Danes, extended from the Tyne, and sometimes even
from the Humber, to the shores of the Frith of Forth. Berwickshire
of course, and Lothian, made part of its northern division, called Bernicia. These counties were often the scene of inroad to the nation
of Scots and Picts, now united under the same monarch, and might
occasionally be occupied by them. But, regularly and strictly speak-

---

* Chaucer's Parsone apologises for not reciting a piece of poetry—

But trusteth wel I am a sotherne man,
I cannot geste, *rom, ram, ruf,* by my letter,
And God wot, rime hold I but litel better.

ing, they, as well as the city of Edinburgh, (Edwins-Burgh,) may be considered as part of England. It acquired in time the name of Lothian, an epithet not only conferred on the counties now comprehended under that term, but also including Berwickshire, afterwards called the March.* The *Lodenensis*, distinguished in the battle of the Standard and elsewhere, were the people of this south-eastern district; and the district appears to have been included amongst those for which, as English possessions, the king of Scotland did homage to his brother of England.† Thus Scotland was, at this early period, deprived of those fertile south-eastern provinces. On the other hand, the south-western frontier of Scotland was enlarged beyond its present bounds by the possession of the ancient British kingdom of Reged, or Cumberland. This was ceded to Malcolm I. by Edmund, after the defeat of Dunmail, the last King of Cumbria. The cause of the cession is obvious. The people of Cumberland were of the same race and manners with those of the Britons of Strath-Clwyde who occupied the opposite frontier of Scotland; and Edmund, who retained but a doubtful sovereignty over Northumberland, would have been still more embarrassed by the necessity of

---

* Simeon of Durham, narrating the journey of the papal legate to Scotland, has these remarkable words,—" Pervenit apud fluvium Tuedam qui Northumbriam et Loidum determinat, in loco qui Rothesburche vocatur."

† Malcolm IV. acknowledged himself vassal to the crown of England for the county of Lothian (among other possessions,) a circumstance which has greatly embarrassed Scottish antiquaries, who are very willing to discover the Comitatus Lodenensis in Leeds or in Cumberland. The truth is, however, that the true meaning rather fortifies the plea of independence. For Lothian, in this enlarged sense, was just the ancient Bernicia, peopled with Saxons or English, and Malcolm did homage for it, not as part of Scotland, but as part of England.

retaining, by garrisons or otherwise, so wild and mountainous a country as the British Reged. By yielding it to Malcolm, he secured a powerful ally capable of protecting the western frontier of Northumberland, and to whose domination the Cumbrians might be the more readily disposed to submit, as it united them with their brethren the Britons of Strath-Clwyde. We have already seen that these districts as far as the Forth, though under the dominion of the Scottish kings, were termed Britain, in opposition to Scotland Proper.

But in the year 1018, Malcolm II. enlarged the eastern limits of his kingdom to the present frontier of Scotland, by a grant from Eadulf, Earl of Northumberland, who ceded to him the whole district of Lothian and Berwickshire to the Tweed. This important addition to his kingdom he certainly continued to retain, although the English historians pretend that Canute carried his arms into Scotland, and penetrated far northwards. If such was the case, his invasion and victory remained without fruits.

What the Scottish kingdom acquired on the eastward in the reign of Malcolm II., was balanced by the loss of Cumberland, which William the Conqueror wrenched from Malcolm Canmore. After this period, although Stephen, in his necessity, ceded Northumberland to Scotland, and, although the English on the other hand frequently held military possession of part of the opposite country, the Borders, with the exception of the Debateable Land to the west, and the town of Berwick on the east, which were constant subjects of dispute, might be considered as finally settled according to the present limits.

While these transactions occurred, other most important changes having taken place both in the interior of South and North Britain, had amalgamated these two grand divisions of the island each into one great kingdom, so that the regions, where they bordered on each other, ceasing to be the residence of independent or tributary states, assumed the character of frontiers, or, as we now term them, of Borders. This important consolidation of England and Scotland, each into a distinct and individual monarchy, took place in both countries nearly about the same period. At least, although the present kingdom of England was formed by the consolidation of the states of the heptarchy rather more early than the Scottish nations were united into one state, the distractions, occasioned by Danish invasions and civil wars, prevented her extending her empire over her northern neighbours. Indeed, the power of England could scarce be said to be wielded by one sovereign with uncontrolled sway, until William the Conqueror had repressed the various insurrections of the Saxons, subjugated for ever the tumultuary Northumbrians, and acquired a consolidated force capable of menacing the kingdom of Scotland. Had this event happened a century sooner, it is probable all Britain would, at that early period, have been united under one monarch. Or had a Scottish monarch existed during the heptarchy, as powerful as Malcolm Canmore at a subsequent ærea, it is possible that he might have pushed his limits much farther to the south than the present Borders, and would probably have secured to Scotland, at least, the countries on the north of the Humber. As it happened, the situation and balanced strength of both countries dictated the present limits.

The Saxons, who gave name to England, and language to both nations, now began to disappear from the stage. The local antiquities which are ascribed to them on the Borders are not numerous:

Their coins, as well as those of the Danish dynasty, are frequently found both in England and Scotland; and cups and drinking horns have been preserved and discovered, which may be referred to this period. But of their architecture the ecclesiastical edifices afford almost the only specimen. The houses, even of their princes, were chiefly formed of wood; and their military system consisted rather in giving battle than in attacking or defending places of strength. Some rude ramparts seem to have encircled their towns for protection against the Danish invaders, and in their own civil dissentions. But castles, whether belonging to kings or chiefs, must have been rare during the Saxon period. No specimens survive on the Border, or even farther south, unless the very singular edifice, called Coningburgh Castle, near Sheffield, be considered as a specimen of Saxon military architecture. The Keep is round instead of being square as usual; and, being supported by six huge projecting buttresses, has a massive, and, at the same time, a picturesque appearance. The mortar is of a kind much more imperfect than that which is used in the Norman buildings, having a mixture of ashes and charcoal and very little lime. In this place the Saxons certainly had a castle, as appears from the name, and tradition points out in its vicinity the *tumulus* of the celebrated Hengist. But it is probable that the Saxon building was repaired and improved by William de Warren the Norman baron, on whom it was bestowed by the Conqueror.

If the Saxons left few examples of their military architecture, they laid the foundation of many splendid ecclesiastical establishments. Once the most fierce, they appear, on their conversion, to have become the most devout nation of Europe. Christianity, though such

advantage should not be named with her inestimable spiritual benefits, brought the arts to Britain in her train. Paulinus, one of the
missionaries, who, by orders of Pope Gregory, had accompanied to
Britain the intrepid Saint Augustin, made great progress in the conversion of Northumberland about the year 625. At Yevering, now
an obscure hamlet, about two miles from Wooller, then the royal
residence of Edwin, King of Northumberland, and his pious spouse,
Ethelburga, Paulinus abode thirty-six days in company with the sovereigns, daily employed in instructing the heathen inhabitants, and
baptizing them in the neighbouring river called the Glen. The first
church which this zealous and successful missionary constructed in
Northumberland was that of Lindisfarne, or Holy Island. It was
formed entirely of wood. But the use of stone was speedily introduced, and the art improving in proportion to the encouragement
which it received, began, during the eighth and ninth centuries, to
assume a more regular and distinct form. The Saxon style of architecture, as it is called with more propriety than that by which the style
that succeeded it is termed Gothic, had now assumed a determined
character. Massive round arches, solid and short pillars, much gloom
and an absence of ornament, mark this original mode of building.
It is also remarkable for a peculiar style of architectural decoration,
described by Mr. Turner in his excellent history of the Anglo-
Saxons, as being a universal diagonal ornament, or zigzag moulding,
" disposed in two ways, one with its point projecting outwards, the
other with its point lying so as to follow the lines which circum-
scribe it, either horizontal, perpendicular, or circular." There is a
curious specimen of this ornament on a door-way in the ruinous part

of the Abbey-Church at Jedburgh,* which looks into the clergyman's garden, which is richly arched with this species of moulding.   In the Chapter-House at the same place may be seen a very perfect specimen of Saxon architecture.

The Saxon historians expatiate with a sort of rapture on the magnificence which Wilfred, Bishop of York, displayed in the erection of a church at Hexham.   It was raised by masons and pargeters brought from Italy, who garnished the building by winding stairs, elevated it into Roman magnificence, and decorated its walls and vaults with pillars, ornamental carving, oratories, and chapels.   Perhaps we may suspect a little exaggeration in this description ; for the same authorities assure us, with little probability, that when Wilfred attempted the conversion of the South Saxons, they were rendered so miserable by famine, that they were in the habit, by forty at a time, to hold each other by the hands and throw themselves into the sea ; and that they were so little able to secure themselves from this evil, that, till instructed by Saint Wilfred, they were ignorant of catching any fish but eels.   A state so grossly savage in Sussex is scarce to be reconciled with a favourable progress in the arts so much farther to the northward.   Still, however, religion appears to have flourished in these savage districts.

Aidan, a monk of Saint Columba's monastery of Iona, was, in 1634, named Bishop of Lindisfarne, or Holy Island, which became soon a renowned seminary.   Melrose, a classical name, owed its original foundation to the same Aidan ; and, as the holy flame spread around and increased, the abbies of Coldingham and Tyningham were

---

* Jedworth, or Jedburgh, was founded A. D. 825.   See *Caledonia*, vol. i. p. 426.

erected. These buildings, like the church of Lindisfarne, were originally fabricated of wood, and afterwards arose in more durable
materials. But of these, and of other Saxon edifices, only fragments
can now be traced. The unsparing fury of the heathen Danes
destroyed almost all the churches on the Borders, and only in a very
few favoured instances can the Saxon architecture be distinguished.
Even its remnants are rendered indistinct by the repairs and additions of later ages. The ancient vaults beneath the present church at
Hexham, which have been constructed chiefly by the use of materials
fetched from some Roman station, as appears from the inscriptions
in Horsley's work, are probably the only part remaining of the
magnificent church of Wilfred. In Holy Island a few diagonal
mouldings and circular arches flatter the fancy of the antiquary that
they may have been part of Saint Cuthbert's original church. At
Jedburgh, the Chapter-House and one highly enriched door-way
have been already noticed. In Kelso Abbey-Church the whole
arches and ornaments of the building are decidedly in the Saxon
style, and its noble, concentrated, and massive appearance, forms one
of the most pure and entire, as well as most favourable, specimens of
that order, which occur on the Scottish Border. The young student of
antiquities is not, however, to set it down as a rule, that, where such
ornaments and arches occur, the edifice exhibiting them is indubitably
as old as Saxon times. The architecture which had arisen among
the Saxons was practised among their successors, not only until the
Gothic, as it is called, was introduced, but even in many later instances, from taste or with a view to variety. It is probable that
the Cumbrian Britons and those of Reged mingled with the Christian religion circumstances expressive of their own ancient man-

ners and customs ; but of this we have little evidence. We may refer, however, to this period, the remarkable monument at Penrith, consisting of two huge stone pillars, richly engraved with hieroglyphics, with a sepulchral stone extended between them. The common tradition terms this the monument of Sir Ewain Cæsarius, a champion who cleared the neighbouring forest of Inglewood of wild beasts.

The edifices upon the Border, dedicated to devotion and peace, arose the more frequently that the good understanding between the English and Scottish nations was for some time only interrupted by occasional and brief wars, bearing little of the character of inveterate hostility which afterwards existed between the sister kingdoms, even in the time of peace. In fact, until the conquest of England by the Normans, and for ages afterwards, each monarch was so earnestly employed in the consolidation of his authority over the mixed tribes to whom it extended, that he had no time for forming schemes of ambition at the expence of his neighbour. If the English frontier regions contained aboriginal Britons, Saxons, Danes, and Normans, the subjects of Scotland were even more miscellaneous. The Picts and Scots had now, indeed, melted down into one people, bearing the latter name ; but the Scoto-Britons of Reged still retained a distinct, though no longer an independent, existence. This was still more the case with the people of Galloway, who, lying more remote from the authority of the kings of Scotland, gave them apparently no other obedience than that which was formerly yielded by the British tribes to the Pendragon, or chief of their federation. There remain to be noticed the Scoto-Saxons, being the descendants of those who, in earlier times, had colonized the northern division of Bernicia, extending from the banks of the Tweed to the Frith of Forth, and skirting on the west the kingdom of Strath-Clwyde. These Saxons were gradually augmented by such of their countrymen as the civil broils of the heptarchy, the invasion of the Danes, and, finally, the sword of the Normans, drove to seek shelter among their northern brethren ; and such was the number of these fugitives, and the influence which they attained at the court of the Scottish monarch, that their language came to be in general use, and at length to supersede the various dialects of the Celtic, which were probably spoken by the other tribes. It cannot but be considered as a very singular phenomenon, that the inhabitants of a ceded province, and that not a large one, should give language to the whole kingdom, although both their original churchmen and royal family were certainly Celtic. But Lothian and the Merse, as the most fertile parts of Scotland, had a natural attraction for her monarchs, and the Saxon language, refined and extended as it must have been by the new emigrants from England, possessed the power of expressing wants and acquisitions unknown to the more simple Celtic nations. It is probable, also, from the expression of Tacitus, that among the various tribes who inhabited the eastern shores of Scotland, particularly about the mouth of the Tay, there might be several of German descent, by whom the Saxon would be readily adopted. Above all, the reader must observe, that, although the Christian missionaries came originally from the Celtic seminary of Iona, yet the large foundations of Lindisfarne, Hexham, Melrose, Coldingham, Jedburgh, and others on the Borders, were endowed by Saxon magnificence, and filled with Saxon monks, who disseminated their language along with their religion through such tribes as still used the British or Celtic tongue. The authority of these Saxon ministers of religion must have been the more prevalent, as they were held to teach a more orthodox doctrine concerning a very important point of controversy—the keeping of Easter, —than their Scottish brethren. On this subject, Queen Margaret, wife of Malcolm Canmore, employed against the Scottish heresy " the sword of the spirit," combating their errors three days, like " St. Helena," says the encomiast, " converting the Jews." Her warlike and royal spouse acted as interpreter on this occasion between his zealous consort and the Scottish clergy, a circumstance which proves that he understood both Saxon and Celtic, she the former language only. It also establishes this fact, that the Lowland Scotch had not yet spread generally through the Celtic tribes, though it did so afterwards.

To the nations already mentioned as subjects of Scotland, must be added the Norman families, who, expelled from England by the various convulsions which took place in that scene of their new conquest, or voluntarily abandoning it in consequence of discovering their services ill recompensed by the Conqueror, were attracted to Scotland by the munificence of Malcolm Canmore. The weak prince, who succeeded that active and enterprising monarch, in vain adopted a different line of policy from his, and laboured to banish from Scotland those foreigners who had settled there under his auspices, —a savage and inhospitable measure by which Donald Bane endeavoured to gain favour with the Scottish tribes, who longed to return to the wild manners of their forefathers. But Alexander I., though himself of a disposition so stern as to acquire the surname of The Fierce, yet, connected with England by marriage, again encouraged the settlement of foreigners in his realm, and the Norman barons,

with their retainers, flocked thither in such numbers, that David I.
addresses his charters to his feal subjects, Franks, English, Scottish,
and Galwegians; and his son Henry classes the inhabitants of his
county of Northumberland into Franks (*i. e.* Normans) and English.

The Normans brought with them their rules of chivalry, their
knowledge of the military art, their terms of honour, and badges of
distinction, and, far the most important, their feudal system of laws.
It is not to be supposed that these were at once imposed on the
Scottish nation at large, as has been erroneously asserted by the ancient historians of that people. But the fiction of law which considered the sovereign as the original source of all property, and which
held the possessors of land by that very act of possession amenable
to his courts, and liable to serve in his armies, rendered the system
acceptable to the king, while the great barons, being each in their
degree invested with the same right and authority within their own
domains, were satisfied to submit to the paramount superiority of
the crown, distant as it was, and feebly exercised, in consideration of
their own direct authority over their vassals being recognised and
acknowledged by the same system. The king, by whom grants of
land were made, and the nobles to whom they were given, had thus
every motive for adopting the feudal form; not to mention that the
Norman Barons, on whom such marks of regal bounty were conferred, would not have accounted that they possessed them securely,
unless they had been expressed in the manner to which the law of
their own country had familiarized them. Thus, while in England,
the feudal law was suddenly imposed in consequence of the Norman conquest, it gradually glided into Scotland, recommended at
once by its own well-modelled and systematic arrangement, by the

interests of the king and of the nobles, and the principle of imitation among the inferior gentry. The clergy, doubtless, lent their
aid to the introduction of the new system, which, while it imposed
no new burthens on their property, gave them at once a firmer and
more durable species of land rights, and sundry facilities for exercising their superior knowledge of law, and of legal documents, at
the expence of the laity. At what time the feudal system was
entirely adopted through the Lowlands of Scotland, it would be difficult to ascertain. We have already seen that the laws of the ancient inhabitants, the customs, as they are called, of the Scots and
Bretts, were in some observance during the temporary usurpation
of Scotland by Edward I., and that it appears to have been the
purpose of that wily monarch, by abolishing these usages, and introducing into the Scottish law an universal observance of the feudal
system, to prepare the way for a more complete union between his
usurped and his hereditary dominions. One leading feature of Celtic manners and laws remained, however, upon the Borders, until
the union of the crowns ; and, in despite of the feudal system with
which it was often at variance, continued to flourish as well in the
southern as in the northern extremities of Scotland. This was the
system of septs, or clan-ship, by which these districts were long distinguished.

The patriarchal government of each tribe, or name, by a single
chieftain, supposed to represent in blood the father from whom the
whole sept claim their original descent, is, of all kinds of government, the most simple and apparently the most universal. It is de-
duced from the most primitive idea of all authority, that right of
command which is exercised by a father over his family. As the

wigwams of the grandchildren arise round the hut of the patriarch, the power of the latter is extended in a wider circumference; and, while the increasing numbers of the tribes bring them into contact, and of course into disputes with other societies of the same kind, this natural HEAD (such is the literal interpretation of the Norman word Chef, or the Celtic Cean) is more extensively useful, as their counsellor in peace and captain in battle. This simple mode of government, very similar to what now exists among the Persian and Hindhu tribes, was universal among the ancient Celtic nations. A confederation of a certain number of these tribes, or clanships, under a government, whether monarchical or popular, composed a Celtic kingdom, or state, but did not alter, or interfere with, the authority exercised by each chief over his own tribe. Thus, ancient Gaul was divided into sixty-four states, comprehending four hundred different tribes; which makes a proportion of about six clans to each federal union. In Britain, in like manner, Cæsar enumerates no less than four kings in the province of Kent alone, by which he must have meant four patriarchal chieftains. That such was the original government of Britain, is sufficiently evident from the system of clanship being found in such perfection in Wales, whose inhabitants, driven into the recesses of their mountains by the Saxons, long maintained with their independence the manners of the ancient British. They acknowledged five royal tribes, and five of churle's blood, to one or other of which each genealogist could refer the pedigree of the subordinate septs. That Ireland, unbroken and untouched by the Romans or Saxons, should have possessed the system of clanship, in all its perfection, cannot be matter of surprise. In the Highlands of Scotland, the system became only extinct in the days of our fathers. And, therefore, as being found in all countries where dialects of the Celtic are spoken, and where their customs continued to be preserved, we must account the system of clanship as peculiar to the Celtic tribes, and unknown to the various invaders of Britain, whether Saxons, Danes, or Normans. As it continued to retain full force upon the Borders, we must hold that it was originally derived from the Celtic inhabitants of the western parts of Valentia, who remained unsubdued by the Saxons, and by those of Reged or the modern Cumberland.

Nor does it at all shake this conclusion, that none of the clans distinguished upon the Borders used the Celtic patronymics common in Ireland, Wales, and the Scottish Highlands, and that we are well assured that several of them are of Saxon or Norman descent. In this case, as in Ireland, the Saxon or Norman settlers seem to have readily conformed to the custom of the native inhabitants, and to have adopted the name and authority of chiefs, with as much readiness and as effectual patriarchal sway, as if they had been descended from Galgacus or Cadwallader. A vague tradition asserts, that the number of Scottish Border clans was eighteen, and of those of the Highlands forty-eight; but I presume there is no genealogist now alive who would undertake to repeat the list. At a late period in the history of the Borders, the Scottish parliament, for the purpose of checking the depredations of these septs, published a "Roll of the Clans that has Captains and Chieftains, on whom they depend ofttimes against the Will of their Landlords, as well on the Borders as Highlands," which, with some brief remarks on Border-names, will be found in the Appendix to this Introduction.*

---

* Appendix, No. XII.

The system of clanship thus established on the western and middle parts of the Border, spread its influence into Berwickshire also; for, although the potent family of Gordon, or of Home, has not, in the strictest sense, been termed a clan, that is, a sept depending entirely upon one patriarchal head, and of which the common people as well as the leaders, bore the same name, yet the heads of the branches of these great families added to their extensive feudal and territorial influence that authority of blood which they exercised over the barons of their own name, as was the case with the Butlers, Giraldines, and other great Norman families settled in Ireland. But on these eastern parts of the marches this clannish attachment was less strong and inviolable, and there are more frequently instances of persons of distinction acting against the head of their family upon occasions of public distraction.* The same thing may be observed on the opposite Borders of England. Northumberland, at least the more level parts of that county, from which the British had been long expelled, was occupied by families of power and distinction, who exercised the same feudal and territorial authority that was possessed by other landholders throughout England. But in the wild and mountainous dales of the Reed, the Tyne, and the Coquet, as well as in the neighbouring county of Cumberland, the ancient British custom of clanship still continued in observance, and the inhabitants acted less under the direction of their landlords than

---

* In the civil wars of Queen Mary, Godscroft (himself a Home) informs us, after enumerating the royalists, that "the Lord Hume did also countenance them, though few of his friends or name were with him, save one mean man, Ferdinando of Broomhouse." —*History of the Douglasses.* Folio Edit. p. 311.

under that of the principal man of their name, corresponding in this respect with the manners of the Cumbrian Britons, from whom they derived their descent. This grand distinction should be heedfully kept in view by the antiquary; because the mode of government, of living, and of making war, adopted by the Borderers on both sides, seems to have been in a great measure the consequence of this prevailing system of clanship.

The simplicity of the system was its first and principal recommendation. The father is the natural magistrate among those of his own family, and his decisions are received with respect, and obeyed without murmur. Allow the fiction (for such it must frequently have been,) that the existing chief was the lineal descendant and representative of the common parent of the tribe, and he became the legitimate heir of his paternal authority. But the consequences of this doctrine led directly to despotism; and indeed it is upon this very foundation that Sir Robert Filmer, the slavish advocate of arbitrary power, has grounded his origin of magistracy. The evil, however great in a more advanced state of society, was not felt by tribes of bounded numbers, and engaged constantly in war. As soldiers, they felt the necessity of submitting absolutely to their leader, while he exerted his authority with tolerable moderation; and, as commanding soldiers, the chief must have felt the hazard of pushing discipline into tyranny. There were also circumstances which balanced the inconvenience of being subjected to the absolute authority of the chieftain. He was not only the legislator and captain and father of his tribe, but it was to him that each individual of the name looked up for advice, subsistence, protection, and revenge.

The article of counsel, it may be supposed, was mutual; for it is reasonably to be presumed, that the chieftain would, in any matter of great moment, use the advice of the persons of most consequence in the clan; as, on the other hand, it was a natural part of his duty to direct and assist them by his opinion and countenance.

The support assigned by the chief to his people was so ample, as to render it questionable whether he could call much proper to himself, excepting his horses and arms. However extensive his territories were, he could use no part of them for his own peculiar profit, excepting just so much as he was able (perhaps by incursions upon the neighbouring kingdom) to stock with sheep and with black cattle, which were consumed in the rude festivals of his castle faster than they could be supplied by the ordinary modes of raising them. The rest of the lands he distributed among his principal friends and relations, by whom they were managed in the same way, that is, partly stocked with cattle for the use of the laird, and partly assigned to be the temporary possessions of the followers. The vassals, or, to speak more properly, the men of name among the kindred, sometimes assisted the revenues of the chief by payment of the various feudal casualties, when he happened to be their feudal superior as well as patriarchal captain. But these seem frequently to have been remitted " in respect of good and acceptable service," and most probably were at all times levied with a very lenient hand.* Payment

* In most collections of deeds respecting the Borders, gifts of nonentry, &c., from the lord Superior to the faulty vassal, are very numerous. But it sometimes happened, that the lands of a powerful chief were possessed by vassals of a clan different from and hostile to his own; and, in that case, the cause of forbearance did not exist. The Beattisons, a very powerful name on the western frontier, at one time possessed all the valley of Esk as the vassals of the Lord Maxwell. As they refused to pay their feudal acknowledgments to that nobleman, he sold the superiority of these lands to the Lord of Buccleuch, who

of rent was totally unknown to the Borders until after James's
accession to the crown of England, and thus the chief's superior
wealth consisted in his extensive herds and flocks. Here also the
inhabitants of the Borders gave token of their Celtic origin. To live
on the produce of their flocks, to be independent of the use of bread,
to eat in quantity the flesh of their cattle, are attributes which Lesley
ascribes to the Borderers in Queen Mary's time, and which also
apply to the Welch and the Irish. On the splendour with which
the chief practised his rude hospitality, much of his popularity,
and of course much of his power, depended. Those who rose to great
consequence were in the custom of maintaining constantly in their
castles a certain number of the younger and more active warriors of
the clan, as we shall have afterwards occasion to notice more particularly. And thus all the chief means of subsistence were expended
in the service of his clan.

Protection was the most sacred duty of a chief to his followers, and
this he was expected to extend in all forms and under almost all circumstances. If one of the clan chanced either to slay a man, or
commit any similar aggression, the chief was expected to defend him
by all means, legal or illegal. The most obvious and pacific was to
pay such fine, or *amende*, or assythement, as it was called, as might
pacify the surviving relations, or make up the feud.[*] This practice

dispossessed and nearly exterminated the rebellious vassals, and retaining a large portion
of their forfeited estates to himself, distributed the rest among the principal persons of
his name.

[*] In the year 1600, Archibald Napier, second son of Sir Alexander Napier of
Merchiston, was way-laid and assassinated by five of the name of Scott, who had a
deadly feud with the unfortunate young man. The present Lord Napier has some
curious correspondence between the father and brother of the slain gentleman, respecting
the assythement offered by the chief in the name of the murderers to atone the quarrel.

of receiving an atonement for slaughter seems also to have been part of the ancient Celtic usages; for it occurs in the Welch laws of Howell Dha, and was the very foundation of the Irish Brehon customs. The vestiges of it may be found in the common law of Scotland to this day. But poor as we have described the Border chief, and fierce as he certainly was by education and office, it was not often that he was either able or disposed to settle the quarrels of his clansmen in a manner so amicable and expensive. War was then resorted to; and it was the duty of the chief and clan who had sustained the injury to seek revenge by every means in their power, not only against the party who had given the offence, but, in the phrase of the time and country, against all his name, kindred, maintainers, and upholders. On the other hand, the chief and clan to whom the individual belonged who had done the offence, were equally bound in honour, by every means in their power, to protect their clansmen, and to retaliate whatever injury the opposite party might inflict in their thirst of vengeance. When two clans were involved in this species of private warfare, which was usually carried on with the most ferocious animosity on both sides, they were said to be at *deadly feud*, and the custom is justly termed by the Scottish parliament most heathenish and barbarous. And the Statute-book expressly states, that the murders, ravage, and daily oppression of the subjects, to the displeasure of God, dishonour of the prince, and devastation of the country, was occasioned partly by the negligence of the landlords and territorial magistrates, within whose jurisdiction the malefactors

---

The brother seems to have declared for revenge, the father appears rather inclined to accommodate the dispute.

dwelt, but chiefly by the chieftains and principal leaders of the clans and their branches, who bore deadly quarrel and sought revenge for the hurt or slaughter of any of their "unhappy race," although done in form of justice, or in recovery of stolen goods. "So that," continues the statute, "the said chieftains, principals of branches, and householders, worthily may be esteemed the very authors, fosterers, and maintainers of the wicked deeds of the vagabonds of their clans or surnames."* In these deadly feuds, the chiefs of clans made war, or truce, or final peace with each other, with as much formality, and as little sincerity, as actual monarchs. Some examples of which the reader will find in the Appendix; and for others he is referred to the account of the private wars between the powerful families of Johnstone and Maxwell, in the end of the sixteenth century, in which each clan lost two successive chieftains. Many battles were fought, and much slaughter committed.†

As the chief was expected to protect his followers, in good and evil, from the assaults of their neighbours, and even from the pursuit of justice, the followers and clansmen were expected, on the other hand, to exhibit the deepest marks of devotion to his interest, never to scruple at his commands when alive, and, in case of his death by violence, to avenge him, at whatever risk to themselves. In the year 1511, Sir Robert Kerr, warden of the Middle Marches, was slain at a Border meeting by three Englishmen. Starkhed, one of the murderers, fled, it is said, nearly as far south as York, and there lived in private and upon his guard. Yet in this place of security he was surprised and murdered by two of Sir Robert Kerr's follow-

---

* Statute, 1594, chap. 211.   † See Minstrelsy of the Scottish Border, Vol. I. p. 260.

ers, who brought his head to their master, by whom, in memorial of their vengeance, it was exposed at the Cross of Edinburgh. These observations may suffice to explain the state of clanship as it existed on the frontier. The cause of the system's subsisting so long was its peculiar adaptation for the purposes of war and plunder, which the relative condition of the two kingdoms rendered in later times the constant occupation of the Borderers. This was not always the case, for there was an early period of history when the hostility between the two kingdoms was neither constant nor virulent.

Until the death of Alexander III. of Scotland, and the extinction of the direct line of succession to the crown opened the way to the ambition of Edward I., there were long continued intervals of peace and amity between England and Scotland. The royal families of each country were united by frequent alliances; and as the possession of extensive domains in England, held of the English crown, frequently obliged the kings of Scotland to attend the court of their brother sovereign, they formed friendships both with the English kings and nobles, which tended to soften the features of hostility when it broke out between the nations. The attachment of Malcolm IV. to Henry II. was so great as to excite the jealousy of his own subjects; and the generosity of Cœur de Lion restored to William of Scotland the pledges of homage which had been extorted from him after his defeat and imprisonment at Alnwick, and converted an impatient vassal into an affectionate and grateful ally. From that period, A.D. 1189, there was an interval of profound peace between the realms for more than a century. During this period, as well as in the preceding reigns, the state of the Border appears to have been in a state of progressive improvement. It was there that David I. chose to establish the monastic institutions whose magnificent remains still adorn that country, the abbies, namely, of Kelso, Melrose, Jedburgh, and Dryburgh. The choise of spots so near the limits of his kingdom (for his possession of some part of the North of England was but precarious) was, perhaps, dictated by the sound policy of ensuring the cultivation of tracks peculiarly exposed to the ravage of the enemy, by placing them under the sacred protection of the church. In this point of view the foundations completely answered the purpose designed ; for it is well argued by Lord Hailes, that while we are inclined to say with the vulgar that the clergy always chose the best of the land, we forget how much their possessions owed their present appearance to the art and industry of the clergy, and the protection which the ecclesiastical character gave to their tenants and labourers, while the territories of the nobles were burnt and laid waste by invaders. If these advantages are taken into consideration, we shall admire, rather than censure, the munificence of David I., and hesitate to join the opinion of his successor, who, adverting to his character of sanctity, purchased, as he deemed it to have been, by his dilapidation of the royal patrimony, observed, sarcastically, that he had proved a sore saint for the crown.

The settlement of these monasteries contributed, doubtless, not a little to the improvement of the country around them ; and the introduction of many Norman families upon the border country must also have had its share in introducing regular law and good order. Under the progressive influence of these changes of property, it seems probable that the Celtic system of clanship would have gradually given way, and that the Borderers would have assimilated their customs and manners to those of the more inland parts of Scotland. But the savage and bloody spirit of hostility which arose from Edward the First's usurpation of the crown of Scotland, destroyed in a few years the improvements of ages, and carried the natives of these countries backward in every art but in those which concerned the destruction of the English and each other. The wars which raged through every part of Scotland in the thirteenth century, were urged with peculiar fury on the Borders. Castles were surprised and taken; battles were won and lost; the country was laid waste on all sides, and by all parties: The patriotic Scotch, like the Spaniards of our own time, had no escape from usurped power but by sacrificing the benefits of civilization, and leading the lives of armed outlaws. The struggle, indeed, terminated in the establishment of national independence; but the immediate effect of the violence which had distinguished it was to occasion Scotland retrograding to a state of barbarism, and to convert the borders of both countries into wildernesses, only inhabited by soldiers and robbers. Many towns, which had begun to arise in the fertile countries of Roxburgh and Berwickshires, were anew ruined. Roxburgh itself, once one of the four principal burghs of Scotland, was so completely destroyed, that its site is now only remembered and pointed out by tradition.

The mode of warfare adopted by the Scots themselves, however necessary and prudent, was destructive to property, and tended to retard civilization. They avoided giving pitched battles, and preferred a wasting and protracted war, which might tire out and exhaust the resources of their invaders. They destroyed all the grain and other resources of their own country which might have afforded relief to the Englishmen, and they viewed with great indifference the enemy complete the work of destruction. In the mean while, they secured their cattle among the mountains and forests, and either watched an opportunity to attack the invaders with advantage, or, leaving them to work their will in Scotland, burst into England themselves, and retaliated upon the enemies' country the horrors which were exercised in their own.* This ferocious, but uncompromising mode of warfare, had been strongly recommended in the rhymes considered a legacy from Robert Bruce to his successors, and which indeed do, at this very day, comprise the most effectual, and almost the only defensive measures, which can be adopted by a poor and mountainous country, when invaded by the overpowering armies of a wealthy neighbour. The concentration of the national forces in woods, mountains, and difficult passages,—the wasting the open country, so as to deprive the enemy of the supplies they might obtain from it,—sudden attacks from ambushes and by night,—a

---

* This extraordinary species of warfare astonished the French auxiliaries, who, under John de Vienne, came to the assistance of the Scottish in the year 1384. They beheld with surprise the Scottish army decline combat, and, plunging into the woods, " destroy," says Froissart, " all as they went, and burn towns, villages, and manors, causing all the men, women, and children to retreat with their cattle into the wild forests, where they knew well that the English could not follow them." Then, while an English army ravaged the country of Scotland, and burned the capital, the Scottish forces burst into Northumberland and Cumberland, wasting, slaying, and burning without mercy, until, in the opinion of the French auxiliaries, they had done more damage in the bishoprics of Durham and Carlisle than all the towns of Scotland were worth. " So the Frenchmen and Scots returned into Scotland the same way they came ; and when they came into Scotland, they found the country destroyed, but the people did set but little thereby, and said how with three or four poles they would soon set up their houses again, and that they had saved much of their cattle in the woods."—*The Cronycle of* FROISSART, vol. II. p. 27. 29.

system of destroying the hostile communications and narrowing their resources, are as distinctly recommended by these homely lines as they were to the Portugueze by the great captain whose conduct and valour achieved their independence. In the following transcript, the modern orthography is preferred :—

> On foot should be all Scottish weir,[*]
> By hill and moss themselves to wear;[†]
> Let wood for walls be bow and speir,
> That enemies do them no dreire.[‡]
> In strait places gar[||] keep all store,
> And burn the plain land them before;
> Then shall they pass away in haste,
> When that they find naething but waste.
> With wiles and wakening on the night,
> And meiklè noises made on height;
> Then shall they turn with great affray
> As they were chased with sword away;
> This is the counsell and intent
> Of good King Robert's testament.
>
> FORDUNI, *Scotichronicon*, vol. II. p. 232.

It followed, from this devastating system of defensive war, that the Scottish were so far from desiring to cover their borders by building strong places or fortresses, that they pulled them down and destroyed them where they already existed. Buchanan has elegantly turned this systematic destruction of their castles into a compliment to the valour of his countrymen;

Nec fossis et muris patriam sed Marte tueri.

But, without disparaging Scottish valour, the motive of leaving their

---

[*] *Weir*—war.   [†] *Wear*—to defend.   [‡] *Dreire*—harm or injury.   [||] *Gar*—cause.

frontier thus open, seems to have been a consciousness that they were greatly surpassed by the English both in the attack and defence of their strong holds;—that if they threw their best warriors into frontier garrisons, they might be there besieged, and reduced either by force or famine; and that the fortresses of which the enemy should thus obtain possession, might afford them the means of maintaining a footing in the country. When, therefore, the Scottish patriots recovered possession of the castles which had fallen into the power of the English, they usually dismantled them. The Good Lord James of Douglas surprised his own castle of Douglas there times, it having been as frequently garrisoned by the English, and upon each occasion he laid waste and demolished it. The military system of Wallace was on the same principle. And, in fine, with very few exceptions, the strong and extensive fortresses, which had arisen on the Scottish Borders in better times, were levelled with the ground during the wars of the thirteenth century. The ruins of the Castles of Roxburgh, of Jedburgh, and of several others which were thus destroyed, bear a wonderful disproportion in extent to any which were erected in subsequent times. Nay, the Castle of Jedburgh was so strongly and solidly constructed, and the Scottish so unskilful in the art of destruction, even where there was no military opposition, that it was thought it could not be destroyed without such time and labour as would render it necessary to impose a tax of two pennies on every hearth in Scotland to defray the expense. But Duke Robert of Albany, then regent, to shun the unpopularity of this impost, defrayed the charge of the demolition out of the crown revenues.

This continued to be the Scottish defensive system for many ages, and, of course, while it exposed invaders to hardships, loss, and want of subsistence, it reduced the frontiers of their own country, for the time, to a waste desart.   Beacons were lighted in such a manner as to signify either the threatened approach, or actual arrival, of the English army.   These were maintained a t Hume Castle, at the Tower of Edgerhope, or Edgerstane, near the sources of the Jed, upon the ridge of the Soltra Hills, at Dunbar, Dunpender (or Trapraine) Law, North-Berwick Law, and other eminences ; and their light was a signal for the Scottish forces to assemble at Edinburgh and Haddington, abandoning to waste and pillage all the southern counties.*   Till the very last occasion of hostility between England and Scotland, this mode of defensive war was resorted to in the latter kingdom.   Cromwell found the Borders in that desolate situation in his campaign of 1650; and, had it not been for the misjudged zeal of the presbyterian ministers, who urged David Lesley to give battle at Dunbar, he must have made a disastrous and disgraceful retreat.†

From this system it followed that most of the Scottish places of strength, even when the abode of great nobles or powerful chiefs,

* Statute 1455. Chap. 28.

† " In the march between Mordington and Coppersmith (Cockburn's Path) we saw not any Scotchman in Eyton, and other places that we passed through ; but the streets were full of Scotch women, pitiful sorry creatures, clothed in white flannel, in a very homely manner.   Very many of them very much bemoaned their husbands, who, they said, were enforced by the lairds of the towns to gang to the muster.   All the men in this town (Dunbar,) as in other places of this day's march, were fled ; and not any to be seen above seven or under seventy years old, but only some few decrepid ones."—*Relation of the fight at Leith, near Edinburgh, &c. published by authority ; printed by Ed. Griffin*, 1650, 4to.

were constructed upon a limited and mean scale. Built usually in some situation of natural strength, and having very thick walls, strongly cemented, they could easily repel the attack of any desultory incursion; but they were neither victualled nor capable of receiving garrisons sufficient to defend them, excepting against a sudden assault. The village, which always almost adjoined to the castle, contained the abodes of the retainers, who, upon the summons of the chieftain, took arms either for the defence of the fortress or for giving battle in the field.* Of these, the greater part were called "kindly tenants," or "rentallers," deriving the former name from the close and intimate nature of their connection with the lord of the soil, from whom they held their little possessions by favour rather than bargain; and the latter from the mode in which their right of possession was constituted, by entering their names in their lord's rental-book. Besides this ready militia, the more powerful chiefs maintained in their castle, and as immediate attendants upon their persons, the more active young gentlemen of their clan, selected from the younger brethren of gentlemen of estate, whose descent from the original stock, and immediate dependance upon the chief, rendered them equally zealous and determined adherents.

---

* Satchells gives a list of the pensioners thus daily maintained in the family of Buccleuch, and distinguishes the lands which each held for his service:—

"That familie they still were valiant men,
No Baron was better served into Britain;
The Barons of Buccleuch they keept at their call
Four and twenty gentlemen in their hall,
All being of his name and kin,
Each two had a servant to wait on them;

These were recompensed by grants of land, in property or lease, which they stocked with cattle or sheep, as their chief did those which he retained in his own hands.

But the castles which held these garrisons, whether constant or occasional, were not of strength, or at least of extent, at all commensurate with the military power of the chiefs who inhabited them. The ruins of Cessford, or of Branxholm, before the latter was modernized, might be considered as on the largest scale of Scottish Border fortresses, and neither could brook comparison with the baronial castles of English families of far less power and influence.

Hume Castle might be reckoned an exception, from its extent and importance. The French king was at one time required to supply a garrison for it, *(Border Hist. p. 571,)* which shews a determination to defend it to the uttermost. But this fortress commanded and protected Berwickshire, a country which, from its wealth and po-

> Before supper and dinner most renowned,
> The bells rung and the trumpet sounded,
> And more than that I do confess,
> They kept four and twenty pensioners;
> Think not I lie, or do me blame
> For the pensioners I can all name;
> There's men alive elder than I,
> They know if I speak truth or lie.
> Ev'ry pensioner a room did gain,
> For service done and to be done,
> This I'le let the reader understand,
> The name of both the men and land,
> Which they possess'd it is of truth,
> Both from the Lairds and Lords of Buckleugh."
> *History of the Name of Scott.*

h

pulation, as well as from the strength of the frontier afforded by the Tweed, early lost the wilder and more savage features of the middle and western Borders. Even in this case it was not without great hazard that the Scottish transgressed their usual rules, by covering this commanding situation with a strong and extensive castle. For Hume Castle was taken by the English after the fatal battle of Pinkie, and again in the year 1570; and being garrisoned by the enemy, afforded, on both occasions, a strong-hold from which they were not easily dispossessed.

The Castle of Caerlaverock, on the western frontier, protected against the English by its situation, appears also to have approached, in size and splendour of architecture, to the dignity of an English fortress; but this fortress also was repeatedly taken by the invaders. The original Castle of Caerlaverock was besieged, taken, and garrisoned by Edward I. in the year 1300. The siege is the subject of a curious French poem preserved in the British Museum, and published in the Antiquarian Repertory. When recovered by Sir Edward Maxwell, during the wars of Robert Bruce, he dismantled it, according to the policy which we have already noticed. The present castle, built on a scale of unusual size and magnificence by the powerful family of Maxwell, was ruined by the Earl of Sussex in the fatal year 1570. Much of the present ruins belong to the seventeenth century; and the castle owes its state of desolation to the successful arms of the Covenanters in 1640.

The extensive ruins of Bruce's ancient castle, on a lake beside Lochmaben, indicate its extent and strength; and, by the Scottish regulations, particular care was enjoined that it should be kept by a " wise and famous gentleman," with four horsemen in constant attendance, who was to discharge the office of steward-depute of Annandale. But Lochmaben Castle was founded before the bloody wars in the fourteenth century, when the Borders were in a state of comparative civilization. Most of the other abodes of the south-western barons, as Closeburn, Spedlin's Castle, Hoddom, Lagg, Amisfield, &c. are towers upon the same plan with those already described.

Even the royal castles on the Border boasted little splendour. That of Newark, a favourite hunting-seat of the kings of Scotland, is merely a large and strong tower, surrounded by a wall of defence, or barnkin. The darksome strength and retired situation of the Hermitage Castle made it long a chosen hold of the Earls of Douglas, and the succeeding branch of the house of Angus, who appear to have fortified it, with little attention indeed to architectural beauty, but so as greatly to improve the natural advantages of its wild sequestered situation. After Hermitage fell into the hands of the crown, it seems usually to have been garrisoned with a few hired soldiers, and was the ordinary residence of the Earls of Bothwell during their power on the Border.

The smaller gentlemen, whether heads of branches of clans, or of distinct families, inhabited dwellings upon a still smaller scale, called Peels, or Bastle-houses. These were surrounded by an inclosure, or barnkin, the wall whereof was, according to statute, a yard thick, six yards in height, surrounding a space of at least sixty square feet.✱ Within this outer work the laird built his tower, with its projecting battlements, and usually secured the entrance by two doors; the outer of grated iron, the innermost of oak clenched with nails. The apart-

---

✱ Statute, 1535.

ments were placed directly above each other, accessible only by a narrow " turnpike" stair, easily blocked up or defended. Sometimes, and in the more ancient buildings, the construction was still more rude: There was no stair at all; and the inhabitants ascended by a ladder from one story to another. Smallholme, or Sandiknow Tower, is one of the most perfect specimens of this species of habitation, which was usually situated on the brow of a rock, or the brink of a torrent; and, like the castle of the chief, had adjacent huts for the reception of those who were called upon to act in its defence. The Castle of Beamerside, still the residence of the ancient family of Haig, is a tower of the same kind, and is still inhabited by the proprietor.

Upon a sudden attack from any small incursive party, these strengths, as they were called, afforded good means of defence. Artillery being out of the question, they were usually attacked with bows, or hagbuts, the discharge of which drove the defenders from the loop-holes and battlements, while the assailants, heaping together quantities of wetted straw, and setting it on fire, drove the garrison from storey to storey by means of the smoke, and sometimes compelled them to surrender. The mode of defence, by stones, arrows, shot, and scalding water, was equally obvious and simple; and, in ordinary cases, by such means of resistance, joined to the strength of the place, and the military disposition of the inhabitants around, who readily rose " to the fray," a desultory attack was easily repulsed. But when, as often happened, the English entered the frontiers with a regular army, supplied with artillery, the lairds usually took to the woods or mountains, with their more active and mounted followers, and left their habitations to the fate of war,* which could seldom do any permanent damage to buildings of such rude and massive construction, as could neither be effectually ruined by fire nor thrown down by force. Hence it is no uncommon circumstance to observe, that the same castles are, in the course of a few years, repeatedly stated to be destroyed in the annals of English invasion. Where, however, it was determined in the English councils to make the Scottish frontiers feel the sword and firebrand, the scale of mischief was immense, and embraced whole districts, while the military inhabitants of the plundered country, so soon as the burst of fury was over, set themselves about to regain by repeated forays, on a smaller scale indeed, but equally formidable from their frequency, a compensation for the property which they had been compelled to abandon to the overpowering force of the invaders. The two most dreadful invasions commemorated in Scottish annals, were the great inroads of the Earl of Hertford in the end of Henry the Eighth's reign, and that of the Earl of Sussex in the twelfth year of Queen Elizabeth.†

While such was the state of the landholder, and even of the noble, upon the Borders, it is natural to enquire into the condition of the towns along the Scottish frontier. It appears they were numerous,

---

* On such occasions it sometimes happened that a few retainers were left as *enfans perdus*, without the means of escape, to hold the tower out to the uttermost, and thus protect the retreat of the laird. This appears from the account given by Patten of the siege of the towers of Anderwick and Thornton by the Lord Protector Somerset, which also contains a minute account of the mode of attacking and defending a Scottish Peel or Bastel-house. Appendix, No. IV.

† See Appendix, No. V.

and, considering the very precarious state of security, full of inhabitants. Dumfries, Jedburgh, and Selkirk, were those of principal note. They were under the same mode of government by their own elective magistrates as the other free boroughs of Scotland, and, on many occasions, maintained their freedom and franchises against the powerful barons in the neighbourhood, with whom they were frequently at feud.* Besides these intestines divisions, they had to be constantly on their guard against the inhabitants of the opposite frontier, to whom their wealth (such as it was) afforded great temptation. It was acquired chiefly by smuggling ; for, as the most rigorous laws in both countries prohibited all mercantile intercourse upon the Borders under high pains, a great contraband trade, both for cattle, horses, salt, fish, and other merchandise, existed upon the frontiers, even till the union of the kingdoms, when most of the southern boroughs of Scotland experienced a great declension, both in wealth and inhabitants, from its being discontinued. Every free burgher was by his tenure a soldier, and obliged, not only to keep watch and ward for the defence of the town, but to march under his

---

* There was a memorable fend betwixt the Laird of Fairnyhirst and the town of Jedburgh, accompanied with some curious circumstances. The chief was attached to the interest of Queen Mary, the burghers of Jedburgh espoused that of King James VI. When a pursuivant, under the authority of the queen, was sent to proclaim that every thing was null which had been done against her, during her imprisonment in Loch-Leven, the provost commanded him to descend from the cross, and, says Bannatyne, "caused him eat his letters, and thereafter loosed down his points, and gave him his wages on his bare buttocks with a bridle, threatening him that if ever he came again he should lose his life." BANNATYNE's *Journal*, p. 243. In revenge of this insult, and of other points of quarrel, Fairnyhirst made prisoners, and hanged ten of the citizens of Jedburgh, and destroyed with fire the whole stock of provisions which they had laid up for the winter.

magistrates, deacons of craft, &c. to join the king's banner when lawfully summoned. They also attended in order of battle and well armed at the warden meetings and other places of public rendezvous on the Borders, had their peculiar gathering words and war-cries, and appear often to have behaved with distinguished gallantry.*

The Border towns were usually strong by situation, as Dumfries upon the Nith, and Jedburgh upon the river of the same name, and were almost always surrounded by some rude sort of fortification, or wall, with gates, or, as they were called in Scottish, ports. But even when these defences were forced by a superior enemy, the contest was often maintained with obstinacy in the town itself, where the height of the houses and narrowness of the streets afforded to brave and determined men the means of resistance, or at least of vengeance. Most of the towns and even villages contained, besides the houses of the poorer inhabitants, bastel-houses, or towers, surrounded with walls, like those which we have described as the habitations of the landed proprietors. The ruins of these are to be seen in most Border villages of antiquity. In that of Darnwick, near Melrose, there is one belonging to a family called Fisher, almost entire. There is another at Jedburgh, which Queen Mary is said to have

---

* The citizens of Jedburgh were so distinguished for the use of arms, that the battle-axe, or species of partizan, which they commonly used, was called a Jeddart-staff, after the name of the burgh. Their bravery turned the fate of the day at the skirmish of the Reedswair, one of the last fought upon the Borders, and their *slogan*, or war-cry, is mentioned in the old ballad which celebrates that event—

> Then rose the slogan with a shout,
> " Fye to it Tynedale"—" Jedburgh's here."

lodged in after her ill-fated expedition to visit Bothwell at Hermitage Castle. These towers were either the abode of the wealthier citizens, or of the neighbouring gentry, who occasionally dwelt within the burgh, and they furnished admirable posts for the annoyance of an enemy, even after they had possessed themselves of the town. Lessudden, a populous village, when burned by Sir Ralph Evers in 1544, contained no less than sixteen strong bastel-houses; and Jedburgh, when taken and burned by the Earl of Surrey, contained six of these strong-holds, with many good houses besides, was twice as large as the town of Berwick, and could have accommodated a garrison of a thousand cavalry. The defence of these towns was very obstinate, the people themselves pulling down the thatch of their houses, and burning it in the streets to stop the progress of their enemies; and the military spirit of the Borderers was such as calls forth the following very handsome compliment from the generous Surrey:—" I assure your Grace (Henry VIII.) that I found the Scots at this time the boldest men and the hottest that ever I saw any nation, and all the *journee* upon all parts of the army they kept us with such continual skirmishes that I never beheld the like. If they could assemble forty thousand as good men as the fifteen hundred or two thousand I saw, it would be a hard encounter to meet them."*

If we turn our eyes from the frontiers of Scotland to those of England, we shall behold a very different scene, indicating, even in these remote provinces, the superior wealth and civilization of the English nation, with that attention to defence which was the natural

---

* Cotton MSS. Calig. B. IV. fol. 29.

consequence of their having something of value to defend. The central marches, indeed, and the extreme verge of the frontier in every direction, excepting upon the east, were inhabited by wild clans as lawless as their northern neighbours, resembling them in manners and customs, inhabiting similar strong-holds, and s ub-sisting, like them, by rapine. The towers of Thirlwall, upon the river Tippal, of Fenwick, of Widdrington, and others, exhibit the same rude strength and scanty limits with those of the Scottish Border chieftains. But these were not, as in Scotland, the abode of the great nobles, but rather of leaders of an inferior rank. Wherever the mountains receded, arose chains of castles of magnificent structure, great extent, and fortified with all the art of the age, belonging to those powerful barons whose names hold so high a rank in English history. The great house of Clifford of Cumberland alone possessed, exclusive of inferior strong-holds, the great and extensive castles of Appleby, Brough, Brougham, Pendragon, and Skipton, each of which formed a lordly residence, as may yet be seen from their majestic ruins. The possessions of the great house of Percy were fortified with equal strength. Warkworth, Alnwick, Bamborough, and Cockermouth, all castles of great baronial splendour and strength, besides others in the interior of the country, show their wealth and power. Raby Castle, still inhabited, attests the magnificence of the great Nevilles, Earls of Westmoreland; and the lowering strength of Naworth shews the power of the Dacres. All these, and many others which might be mentioned, are so superior to edifices of the same kind in Scotland, as to verify the boast, that there was many a dog-kennel in England to which the

101161089188

tower of a Scottish Borderer was not to be compared.* Yet when Naworth or Brougham Castles are compared with the magnificence of Warwick and of Kenilworth, their savage strength, their triple rows of dungeons, the few and small windows which open to the outside, the length and complication of secret and subterranean passages, shew that they are rather to be held limitary fortresses for curbing the doubtful allegiance of the Borders, and the incursions of the Scottish, than the abodes of feudal hospitality and baronial splendour.

The towns along the English frontier were, in like manner, much better secured against incursions than those of the opposite Borders. The necessity of this had been early taught them. In the reign of Edward I., a wealthy burgess of Newcastle was made prisoner in his own house by a party of Scottish moss-troopers, carried into Scotland, and compelled to ransom himself. This compelled the inhabitants to fortify that city.† The strength and importance of Berwick, often won and lost during the fourteenth century, induced the English to bestow such expence and skill in fortifying it, that, after the year 1482, it remained as a gate between the kingdoms, barred against the Scottish, but through which the English could at pleasure make irruption. A strong garrison was maintained in that city, ready at all times for service; and, to have kept Berwick-upon-Tweed, was of itself a sufficient praise for a military man, and sums

---

* See *Cabala*, p. 160.

† Chorographia, or a Survey of Newcastle-upon-Tyne, republished by the Antiquarian Society of that city.

up, in a minstrel ballad, the character of Harry Hotspur himself.* When garrisons of regular troops were lodged, as was usually the case, in the royal castle of Norham, and Lord Grey's baronial castle of Wark, with smaller parties in those of Etal, Ford, Cornhill, and Twizell, the course of the Tweed, where it divides the kingdoms, was well protected from invasion; and the necessary siege of one or other of this chain of fortresses usually found the Scottish arms such employment, that, ere they could advance into the interior of Northumberland, the array of England was collected and combined for the defence of her frontier. Carlisle, strong and skilfully fortified, having besides a castle of great antiquity and strength, was to the English west marches what Berwick was on the east, a place of arms and a rallying-point. The crown appears frequently to have maintained garrisons there, besides the retinue which was assigned to the wardens, as also at Askerton in Bewcastle, Naworth, and other places of strength. Hexham, in the centre of the Border line, was

---

* In the old song of the Battle of Otterbourne, Hotspur is thus eulogized:

Sir Henry Percye in the New Castell lay,
   I tell ye withouten drede,
He had been a march-man all his dayes,
   And kept Berwicke upon Tweed.

Sir Ralph Evers, a Border hero of later date, who was slain in the battle of Ancrummoor, receives a similar compliment from the minstrel by whom he was celebrated—

And now he has in keeping the town of Berwicke,
   The town was ne'er so well keepit I wot;
He maintain'd law and order along the Border,
   And ever was ready to prikke the Scot.

also fortified, so that if any considerable body of the Scottish forces should penetrate through the wastes of Reedsdale and Tynedale, they might still find an obstacle in their passage.

But, although these precautions served to protect the English frontier from those extensive scenes of inroad and desolation which their arms sometimes inflicted on Scotland, and in so far afforded them defence, yet the evils of the desultory war carried on by small parties of the enemy, who made sudden irruptions into particular districts, laid all waste, and returned loaded with spoil, were not to be guarded against. If the waste committed by the English armies was more widely extended and generally inflicted, the continual and unceasing *raids* of the Scottish Borderers were scarcely less destructive. The English, if better defended by castles and garrisons, afforded, from the superior wealth of the country, stronger temptation to their free-booting neighbours, and gain is a surer spur to adventures of this kind than mere revenge. The powerful Earl of Northumberland, writing to Henry VIII., complains, that from his house at Warkworth he sees the horizon enlightened by the burning hamlets, which the Scottish marauders had pillaged and fired. Such were the frequent signals of invasion—

> ——————— at whose sight
> So oft the yeoman had in days of yore,
> Cursing his perilous tenure, wound the horn ;
> And warden from the castle-tower rung out
> The loud alarm-bell, heard far and wide.
> *Madoc*, p. 359.

The tenure of Cornage, alluded to by the poet in these beautiful lines, was well known on the English Borders, as well as on the

Marches of Wales, to which the verses refer. The smaller barons usually held their lands and towers for the service of winding a horn, to intimate the approach of a hostile party. An alarm of this sort, and its consequences, Æneas Silvius witnessed on his passing through Northumberland in his road to Scotland, in the character of a legate, in the year 1448.

" There is a river, (the Tweed) which spreading itself from a high mountain, parts the two kingdoms; Eneas having crossed this in a boat, and arriving about sunset at a large village, went to the house of a peasant, and there supped with the priest of the place and his host. The table was plentifully spread with large quantities of poultry and geese, but neither wine nor bread was to be found there, and all the people of the town, both men and women, flocked about him as to some new sight; and as we gaze at Negroes or Indians, so did they stare at Eneas, asking the priest where he came from, what he came about, and whether he was a Christian. Eneas, understanding the difficulties he must expect on this journey, had taken care to provide himself at a certain monastery with some loaves, and a measure of red wine, at sight of which they were seized with greater astonishment, having never seen wine or white bread. Women with child came up to the table with their husbands, and after handling the bread and smelling the wine, begged some of each, so that it was impossible to avoid distributing the whole among them. The supper lasted till the second hour of the night; the priest and host, with all the men and children, made the best of their way off, and left Eneas. They said they were going to a tower a great way off for fear of the Scots, who, when the tide was out, would come over the river and plunder; nor could they with all his intreaties by any means be pre-

vailed on to take Eneas with them, nor any of the women, though
many of them were young and handsome, for they think them in no
danger from an enemy, not considering violence offered to women as
any harm. Eneas therefore remained alone for them with two servants
and a guide, and 100 women, who made a circle round the fire, and
sat the rest of the night without sleeping, dressing hemp and chatting
with the interpreter. Night was now far advanced, when a great
noise was heard by the barking of dogs, and screaming of the geese.
All the women made the best of their way off, the guide getting away
with the rest, and there was as much confusion as if the enemy was
at hand. Eneas thought it more prudent to wait the event in his
bed-room, (which happened to be a stable,) apprehending if he went
out he might mistake his way and be robbed by the first he met.
And soon after the women came back with the interpreter, and
reported there was no danger, for it was a party of friends, and not of
enemies, that were come."

To prevent these distressing inroads, the English warden, Lord
Wharton, established a line of communication along the whole line
of the Border, from Berwick to Carlisle, from east to west, with setters
and searchers, sleuth-hounds, and watchers by day and night.*
Such fords as could not be conveniently guarded, were, to the
number of thirty-nine, directed to be stopped and destroyed, meadows
and pastures were ordered to be enclosed that their fences might
oppose some obstacle to the passage of marauders, and narrow passes
by land were appointed to be blocked up or rendered unpassable

* See Articles devised at Newcastle in the 6th of Edward VI. Border Laws, Appendix.

All these precautions, while they shewed the extent of the evil, did not, however anxiously considered and carefully enforced, produce, in any remarkable degree, the good effects which might have been expected. Indeed, the state of the population on either side of the frontier had become such, that to prevent these constant and reciprocal incursions was absolutely impossible, without a total change on their manners and habits of life. And this leads us to take a brief review of the character and manners of the Borderers on either side.

Lesley, bishop of Ross, has given us a curious chapter on the manners of the Borderers of Scotland, a translation whereof the reader will find in the Appendix, No. VI. Contrary to the custom of the rest of Scotland, they almost always acted as light-horsemen, and used small active horses accustomed to traverse morasses, in which other cavalry would have been swallowed up. Their hardy mode of life made them indifferent to danger, and careless about the ordinary accommodations of life. The uncertainty of reaping the fruits of their labour, deterred them from all the labours of cultivation; their mountains and glens afforded pasturage for the cattle and horses, and when these were driven off by the enemy, they supplied the loss by reciprocal depredation. Living under chiefs by whom this predatory warfare was countenanced, and sometimes headed, they appear to have had little knowledge of the light in which their actions were regarded by the legislature; and the various statutes and regulations made against their incursions, remained in most cases a dead letter. It did indeed frequently happen that the kings, or governors of Scotland, when the disorders upon the Border reached to a certain height, marched against these districts with an overpowering force, seized on the persons of the chiefs, and sent them to distant prisons in the centre of the kingdom, and executed, without mercy, the inferior captains and leaders. Thus, in the year 1529, a memorable æra for this sort of expeditious justice, James V., having first committed to ward the Earl of Bothwell, the Lords Home and Maxwell, the Lairds of Buccleuch, Fairnihirst, Johnstone, Polwarth, Dolphington, and other chiefs of clans, marched through the Borders with about eight thousand men, and seizing upon the chief leaders of the moss-troopers, who seem not to have been aware that they had any reason to expect harm at their sovereign's hands, executed them without mercy. Besides the celebrated Johnie Armstrong of Gillnockie, to whom a considerable part of the English frontier paid black-mail, or protection-money, the names of Piers Cockburn of Henderland, Adam Scott of Tushielaw, called the King of the Border, and other marauders of note, are recorded as having suffered on this occasion. And although this, and other examples of severity, had the effect for the time, as the Scottish phrase is, of " dantoning the thieves of the Borders, and making the rush-bush keep the cow," yet this course not only deprived the kingdom of the assistance of many brave men, who were usually the first to endure or repel the brunt of invasion, but it also diminished the affections of those who remained ; and a curious and middle state of relation appears to have taken place between the Borderers on each side, who, as they were never at absolute peace with each other during the cessation of national hostilities, seem, in like manner, to have shunned engaging in violent and sanguinary conflicts, even during the time of war. The English Borderers, who were in the same manner held aliens to the civilized part of the country, insomuch that, by the regulations of the corporation of Newcastle, no burgess could take to his apprentice a youth from the dales of Reed or Tyne made common cause with those of Scotland, the allegiance of both to their proper country was much loosened; the dalesmen on either side seem to have considered themselves in many respects as a separate people, having interest of their own, distinct from, and often hostile to, that of the country to which they were nominal subjects. This gave rise to some singular features in their history.

In the first place, this indifference to the national cause rendered it the same thing to the Borderers whether they preyed upon the opposing frontier, or on their own countrymen. The men of Tynedale and Reedsdale, in particular, appear to have been more frequently tempted by the rich vales of the Bishoprick of Durham, and other districts which lay to the southward, than by the rude desolation of the Scottish hills. Their wild manners are thus described in the Chorographia, or Survey of Newcastle, first published in 1549.

"There is in many dales, the chief are Tinedale and Reedsdale, a countrey that William the Conquerour did not subdue, retaining to this day the ancient laws and customs, (according to the county of Kent) whereby the lands of the father is equally divided at his death amongst all his sonnes. These Highlanders are famous for thieving; they are all bred up and live by theft. They come down from these dales into the low countries, and carry away horses and cattell so cunningly, that it will be hard for any to get them or their cattell, except they be acquainted with some master thiefe, who for some mony (which they call saufey-mony) may help them to their stoln goods, or deceive them.

"There is many every yeare brought in of them into the goale

k

of Newcastle, and at the assizes are condemned and hanged, sometimes twenty or thirty. They forfeit not their lands, (according to
the tenure in gravelkind) the father to bough, the sonne to the
plough.

"The people of this countrey hath had one barbarous custome
amongst them ; if any two be displeased, they expect no lawe, but
bang it out bravely, one and his kindred against the other and his ;
they will subject themselves to no justice, but in an inhumane and
barbarous manner fight and kill one another ; they run together in
clangs (clans) as they terme it, or names.

" This fighting they call their feids, or deadly feides, a word so
barbarous that I cannot express it in any other tongue. Of late, since
the union of both kingdoms, this heathenish bloody custom is repressed,
and good laws made against such barbarous and unchristian misde-
meanours and fightings."

The Scottish Borderers seem to have been, in all respects, as little
amenable to the laws of their country, and as little disposed to respect
the rights of their countrymen as the Dalesmen of Northumberland.
Their depredations not only wasted the opposite frontier of England,
but extended through the more civilized parts of Scotland, and
even into Lothian itself; and it is singular enough, that a Scottish
lord chancellor seems to have had no more effectual mode of
taking vengeance on them than by writing a poem of exprobation.*

---

* See Maitland's Complaint against the Thieves of Liddesdale, in Pinkerton's Scottish Poems ; and a copy, somewhat different, in the Minstrelsy of the Scottish Border,
vol. I.

> Of Liddesdale, the common thieves
> Sae pertly steilis now and reives,

They entered readily into any of the schemes of the English Borderers, and we find them contributing their numbers to swell the army with which the unfortunate Earls of Westmoreland and Cumberland, in the twelfth year of Queen Elizabeth, as well as upon other occasions when public commotion gave hope of plunder.* But their allegiance hung much more loosely about them than this would imply; for not only did they join the English Borderers in their exploits against the English government, but upon any turn of affairs which was favourable to the arms of England, they readily took assurance, as it is called, or allied themselves with that kingdom, and assisted them with their forces in laying waste their native country.

> That nane may keep
> Horse, nolt, or sheep,
> Nor yet dare sleep
> For their mischievis.
> *   *   *   *   *
> These thieves have well nigh harried hail
> Ettricke-forest and Liddesdale;
> Now they are gane
> In Lothian
> And sparis nane
> That they will wale.

The poet enumerates the principal leaders of this banditti, each of whom, he says, had a *To-name*, a soubriquet, that is, or *nomme de guerre*, to distinguish him from others of the same clan. He mentions Will of the Laws, Hob of the Shaws, the Laird's Jock, John of the Syde, and other merry-men, whose fame is not yet quite forgotten on the Border.

* Sir Ralph Sadler writes to the Secretary Cecill, " My said servant told me, that the rebells ar abouts the number of 3ᵐ (3000), whereof 7ᶜ (700) horsemen, of the which I here say there be 4 or 5ᶜ (4 or 500) of the thieves and outlawes of Tyndale, Riddesdale, and also of Tividale, both English and Scottish theves together, and the residue of the saide 3ᵐ are footemen.''

This was particularly the case with the Borderers who inhabited the *Debateable Land*, as it was called, a considerable portion of ground upon the west marches, the allegiance of whose inhabitants was claimed by both parties, and rendered to neither. They were outlawed to both nations, and readily made incursions upon either, as circumstances afforded the best prospect of plunder.* The inhabitants of Liddesdale, also comprehending the martial clans of Armstrong, Elliot, and others, were apt, on an emergency, to assume the red cross, and for the time became English subjects. They had indeed this to plead for their conduct, that the sovereigns of Scotland had repeatedly abandoned them to the vengeance of English retaliation, on account of hostilities against that country, which their own monarchs were unable to punish.† These clans, with the Rutherfords, Crossers, Turnbulls, and others, were the principal instruments

---

* The Debateable Land (a perpetual source of contention between the kingdoms) was a small tract of ground, inhabited by the most desperate outlaws of both nations, lying between the rivers Sark and Esk. In 1552, it was divided by commissioners of both nations, the upper or more western part being assigned to Scotland, and the lower portion to England, in all time coming.

† By a convention, dated at Berwick in the year 1528, it is declared lawful for the King of England to proceed by letters of marque, authorizing his wardens and other officers to proceed against the inhabitants of Liddesdale to their slaughter, burning, hership, robbing, reiving, despoiling, and destruction, till full redress was obtained of the wrongs complained of. But it is provided, that the English shall not besiege the house or castle of Hermitage, or appropriate any part of Liddesdale, or accept of the homage of any of its inhabitants being Scotchmen by birth. The same singular mode of coercion was to be competent to the King of Scotland for the injuries committed by the clans of Leven, and inhabitants of the tract of country between the Crissep, the Liddell, and that stream. Each monarch might prevent this hostile mode of procedure against his subjects, by offered redress and satisfaction, by the 11th of January, 1748-9, or within forty days thereafter.—RYMER's *Fœdera*, p. 276.

of the devastation committed in Scotland in the year 1445.* They expiated this fault, however, by another piece of treachery towards their English allies, when, seeing the day turn against them at Ancrummoor, these assured Borderers, to the number of 700 men, suddenly flung away their red crosses, and, joining their countrymen, made great and pitiless slaughter among the flying invaders.

It followed, as another consequence of the relations which the Borderers held with each other, that, as they were but wavering in allegiance to their own country, so their hostilities upon the other, though constant and unremitted, were seldom marked by a sanguinary character. The very unremitted nature of the predatory war between them gradually introduced rules, by which it was modified and softened in its features. Their incursions were marked with the desire of spoil, rather than that of slaughter. Indeed, bloodshed was the rather avoided, as it uniformly demanded revenge, and occasioned a deadly feud between two clans; whereas the abstraction of property was only considered as a trivial provocation. As we have noticed the fury with which they revenged the former injury, we may here give an instance of the care which they took to avoid it. When the discomfited Earls of Northumberland and Westmoreland entered Liddesdale, after the dispersion of their forces in the twelfth of Queen Elizabeth, they were escorted by Black Ormiston, and other Borderers. Martin Elliot of the Preakin Tower, who was attached to the Regent Murray, raised his clan to intercept their passage; but when both parties had met, and dismounted from their horses to fight out their quarrel, Elliot said to Ormiston, " he would be sorry to enter

* See Appendix, No. IV.

into deadly feud with him by bloodshed, but he would charge him
and the rest before the regent for keeping of the rebels ; and if he did
not put them off the country the next day, he would do his worst
against them ;" and thus they parted on a sort of composition.*
Patten, in describing the English Borderers, gives many insinuations
that their hostilities against their Scottish neighbours were not of a
resolved or desperate nature.   They wore, he observes, handkerchiefs
on their arms, and letters embroidered on their caps, which he hints
enabled them to maintain a collusive correspondence with the Scottish
who bore similar cognizances.   He said they might be sometimes
observed speaking familiarly to the Scottish prickers, within less than
spear's length ; and when they saw themselves noticed, they began to
charge each other, but so far from serious was their skirmish, that it
rather resembled countrymen playing at bar, or novices in a fencing-
school.   Lastly, he affirms that they attended much more to making
prisoners than to fighting, so that few brought home less than one
captive, and many six or seven.   Their captains and gentlemen, this
censor admits, are men of good service and approved prowess; but
he seems to doubt the fidelity of the northern prickers, who served
under them.

   Yet these men, who might thus be said to bear but dubious
allegiance to their country, were, of all others, the most true of faith
to whatever they had pledged their individual word: If it happened
that any of them broke his troth, he who had sustained the wrong
displayed, at the first public meeting upon the Borders, a glove on
the point of a lance, and proclaimed him a perjured and mansworn

---

* Cabala.

traitor. This was accounted an insult to the whole clan to which the culprit belonged. If his crime was manifest, there were instances of his being put to death by his kinsmen; but if the accusation was unfounded, the stain upon the honour of the clan was accounted equal to the slaughter of one of its members, and, like that, could only be expiated by deadly feud. Under the terrors of this penalty, the degree of trust that might be reposed in the most desperate of the Border outlaws, is described by Robert Constable, in his account of an interview with the banished Earl of Westmoreland and his unfortunate followers. They desired to get back into England, but were unwilling to trust their fortune without sure guides. "I promised," said Constable, " to get them two guides that would not care to steale, and yet they would not bewray any man that trusts in them for all the gold in Scotland or France. They are my guides and outlaws; if they would betray me they might get their pardons, and cause me to be hanged, but I have tried them ere this."*

This strict observance of pledged faith tended much to soften the rigours of war; for when a Borderer made a prisoner, he esteemed it wholly unnecessary to lead him into actual captivity or confinement. He simply accepted his word to be a true prisoner, and named a time and place where he expected him to come to treat about his ransom. If they were able to agree, a term was usually assigned for the payment, and security given; if not, the prisoner surrendered himself to the discretion of his captor. But where the interest of both parties pointed so strongly towards the necessity of mutual accommodation, it rarely happened that they did not agree upon

---

* Sadler's Letters, vol. II.

terms. Thus, even in the encounters of these rude warriors on either side, the nations maintained the character of honour, courage, and generosity assigned to them by Froissart. " Englishmen on the one party, and Scotsmen on the other party, are good men of war ; for when they met, there is a hard fight without sparing ; there is no hoo (*i. e.* cessation for parley) between them, as long as spears, swords, axes, or daggers will endure ; but they lay on each upon other, and when they be well beaten, and that the one party hath obtained the victory, they then glorify so in their deeds of arms, and are so joyful that such as be taken they shall be ransomed ere they go out of the field ; so that shortly each of them is so content with other, that at their departing courteously, they will say, ' God thank you.' But in fighting one with another, there is no play, nor sparing."✱

Of the other qualities and habits of the Borderers we are much left to form our own conjectures. That they were a people of some accomplishment, fond of the legends of their own exploits, and of their own rude poetry and music, is proved by the remains still preserved of both. They were skilful antiquaries, according to Roger North, in whatever concerned their own bounds. Lesley gives them the praise of great and artful eloquence when reduced to plead for their lives ; also that they were temperate in food and liquors and rarely tasted those of an intoxicating quality. Their females caught the warlike spirit of the country, and appear often to have mingled in battle. Fair Maiden Lilliard, whose grave is still pointed out upon the field of battle at Ancram-moor, called, from her name, Lilliard's Edge, seems to have been a heroine of this descrip-

---

✱ Berner's Froissart, Edit. 1812. vol. II. p. 396.

tion. And Hollinshed records them at the conflict fought near Naworth, (A. D. 1570) between Leonard Dacres and Lord Hunsdon; the former had in his company " many desperate women, who there gave the adventure of their lives, and fought right stoutly. This is a change in the habits of the other sex which can only be produced by early and daily familiarity with scenes of hazard, blood, and death. The Borderers, however, merited the devoted attachment of their wives, if, as we learn, one principal use of the wealth they obtained by plunder was to bestow it in ornamenting the persons of their partners.

It may be easily supposed, that men living in so rude a state of society, had little religion, however well they might be stored with superstition. They never told their beads, according to Lesley, with such devotion as when they were setting out upon a marauding party, and expected a good booty as the recompense of their devotions. The various religious houses, which the piety or the superstition of an earlier age had founded in these provinces, gradually ceased to overawe, by their sanctity, the spirits of the invaders; and in the history of the mutual incursions of the two hostile nations, we read repeatedly of their being destroyed and laid waste. Thus the administration of religious rites became irregular and unusual in these wild districts. Of this negligence some traces still remain. The churches on the English Border are scantily endowed, and many of them are ruinous. In some parishes there is no house for the incumbent to inhabit, and in others no church for divine service. But these are only the scars of ancient wounds; for in former times the condition of these countries, as to spiritual matters, was more extraordinary and lamentable. In the dales of Esk, Euse, and Liddell, there were no

1

churchmen for the ordinary celebration of the rites of the church. A monk from Melrose, called, from the porteous or breviary which he wore in his breast, a *book-a-bosom*, visited these forlorn regions once a-year, and solemnized marriages and baptisms. This is said to have given rise to a custom called by tradition, *hand-fasting*, by which a loving couple, too impatient to wait the tardy arrival of this priest, consented to live as man and wife in the interim. Each had the privilege, without loss of character, to draw back from the engagement, if, upon the arrival of the holy father, they did not think proper to legitimate their cohabitation according to the rites of the church. But the party retreating from the union was obliged to maintain the child, or children, if any had been the fruits of their union.

It would seem that the opposite valleys of Redesdale and Tynedale were better supplied with persons (such as they were) who took upon them the character of churchmen. There is extant a curious pastoral monition of Richard Fox, Bishop of Durham, dated sometime between the years 1490 and 1498, in which, after setting forth the various enormities of theft, robbery, rapine, and depredation committed by the dalesmen of the Reed and Tyne, and the neighbouring district, not only without shame and compunction, but as the ordinary and proper business of their lives, after stating that they were encouraged in these enormities by the king's officers of justice, and patronised either for kindred's or name's sake, or for the lucre of gain, by the powerful and noble of these districts, the prelate proceeds to describe a sort of ghostly comforters and abettors who were found among them, irregular and dissolute churchmen suspended from their holy office for misconduct, or lying under the sentence of excommunication, so ignorant of letters, that they did not even understand the service of the church which they had recited for years, and with them laymen, never ordained, who yet took upon themselves the sacred character of the priesthood. These men, proceeds the monition, dressed in tattered, foul, and sordid vestments, not only unfit for the ministers of Heaven, but even for decent society among men, presume and take upon them, not only in hallowed and dedicated places, but in such as are profane, interdicted, unholy, and defaced by ruins, to administer the rites and sacraments of the church to the thieves, robbers, murderers, and depredators before mentioned, and that without exhorting them to restitution or repentance, expressly contrary to the rules of the church, and to the great danger of precious souls, and scandal of Christianity. The Bishop instructs his suffragans to direct against the robbers and their abettors, whether spiritual or temporal, his pastoral monition to restitution and repentance, to be followed by the thunders of excommunication in case it were contemned by the offenders. It would seem several of the Borderers had accordingly been excommunicated; for, by a rescript, dated at Norham Castle, 5th September, 1498, the same prelate releases from the spiritual sentence certain persons of the clans of Charleton, Robson, Tod, Hunter, and others, who had professed penitence for their misdeeds, and submitted, in all humility, to his paternal chastisement. The penance annexed to their release from spiritual censures was of a singular kind, but illustrates their ordinary costume and habits of life. They are required to renounce the use of the *jack* and head-piece, and to ride upon no horse which shall exceed, in ordinary estimation, the sum of six shillings and eightpence. Moreover, they are enjoined, when they shall enter any church, chapel, or cemetery in the territory of Redesdale or Tynedale, to lay aside, upon their entrance, every offensive weapon exceeding one cubit in length, and to hold speech with no one while within these hallowed precincts, excepting the curate or ministering priest of the said church or chapel, all under penalty of the greater excommunication. Mr. Surtees justly observes, that the reclaiming of these Borderers must be ascribed to the personal influence of this able and worthy prelate; but there is ample reason to believe that no radical cure was wrought either in freebooters at large, or in the manners of those irregular and uncanonical churchmen, who, attending them as Friar Tuck is said to have done upon Robin Hood, partook in their spoils, and mingled with the reliques of barbarism the rites and ceremonies of the Christian church.* The injunction of laying aside offensive weapons, and keeping silence in the church and its precincts, was to prevent the sacred place from becoming the scene of those bloody quarrels, which usually occurred whenever or wheresoever the members of clans, between which a deadly feud existed, chanced to meet together. How late the savage customs which rendered such regulations necessary, continued to last among the Northumbrians is evident from some passages in the Life of the truly pious and Christian teacher, Bernard Gilpin, who having a pastoral charge in these wild countries, in the reign of Queen Elizabeth, laboured unremittingly to soften and civilize the yet wilder manners of the inhabitants.

The biographer of this venerable man, after stating the fierce

---

* See the History of Durham, by Mr. Surtees, p. lxii. Also the last edition of the Minstrelsy of the Scottish Border, where the record of the excommunication and release is printed at length, from the communication of that accurate and indefatigable antiquary.

usage of deadly feud which often engaged two clans in much bloodshed, on account of some accidental quarrel, proceeds thus: "It
happened that a quarrel of this kind was on foot when Mr. Gilpin
was at Rothbury, in those parts. During the two or three first days
of his preaching, the contending parties observed some decorum,
and never appeared at church together; at length, however, they
met. One party had been early at church, and just as Mr. Gilpin
began his sermon, the other entered. They stood not long silent.
Inflamed at the sight of each other, they begin to clash their weapons,
for they were all armed with javelins and swords, and mutually
approach. Awed, however, by the sacredness of the place, the
tumult in some degree ceased. Mr. Gilpin proceeded, when again
the combatants began to brandish their weapons and draw towards
each other. As a fray seemed near, Mr. Gilpin stepped from the
pulpit, went between them, and addressed the leaders, put an end to
the quarrel for the present, but could not effect an entire reconciliation. They promised him, however, that, till the sermon was over,
they would make no more disturbance. He then went again into the
pulpit, and spent the rest of the time in endeavouring to make them
ashamed of what they had done. His behaviour and discourse
affected them so much, that at his farther entreaty, they promised to
forbear all acts of hostility while he continued in the country. And
so much respected was he among them, that whosoever was in fear of
his enemy, used to resort where Mr. Gilpin was, esteeming his
presence the best protection.

" One Sunday morning, coming to a church in those parts before
the people were assembled, he observed a glove hanging up, and was
informed by the sexton that it was meant as a challenge to any one

that should take it down. Mr. Gilpin ordered the sexton to reach it him; but upon his utterly refusing to touch it, he took it down himself, and put it in his breast. When the people were assembled, he went into the pulpit, and before he concluded his sermon, took occasion to rebuke them severely for these inhuman challenges. ' I hear,' said he, ' that one among you hath hanged up a glove even in this sacred place, threatening to fight any one who taketh it down; see, I have taken it down; and pulling out the glove, he held it up to the congregation, and then showed them how unsuitable such savage practices were to the profession of Christianity, using such persuasives to mutual love as he thought would most affect them."*

The venerable preacher had his reward, for even the freebooter who stole his horses, returned them as soon as he understood to whom they belonged, not doubting that the foul fiend would have carried him off bodily, had he wilfully injured Bernard Gilpin. But it was long ere the effects of the northern apostle's precepts brought forth in that rude country fruits meet for repentance.

Leaving the manners of the Borderers, it is now proper to notice the measures of policy adopted for exercising, in some sort, the royal authority in districts which so many circumstances combined to render lawless; and that whether for the protection of each nation against the aggressions of the other during peace, or for repelling more open invasion during the time of war, or for regulating the conduct and appeasing the feuds of the inhabitants amongst themselves.

---

* Life of Bernard Gilpin, 1753, p. 178.

As every thing was military upon the Borders, those important duties were intrusted to officers of high rank, holding special commissions from the crown of either country, and entitled wardens, or guardians of the marches. There were sometimes two, sometimes three in number on each side, for the division of the Borders into east, west, and middle marches, did not prevent the middle marches being occasionally put under the charge of the same warden who governed those on the east or west. The kings of Scotland, compelled by circumstances to yield to the great nobles and powerful chiefs whatever boons they chose to exact of them, usually deposited the charge of warden with some nobleman or chieftain who possessed great personal weight and influence in the districts submitted to his jurisdiction. It is needless to point out the impolicy of this conduct, since the chiefs thus invested with high powers and jurisdiction were often the private encouragers of those disorders which it was their business, as wardens, to have suppressed, and hence their authority was only used to oppress their private enemies, while they connived at the misconduct of their own clansmen and allies. But this was the effect of the weakness, rather than of the blindness, of the Scottish sovereigns. Even the timid Albany, regent during the minority of James V., saw the evil, and endeavoured to secure impartial administration of justice on the frontiers, by naming a gallant French knight, Anthony D'Arcy Sieur De La Bastie, to the wardonry of the east marches. But the family of Home being incensed to see the office conferred on a stranger which they were wont to consider as proper to the head of their own house, in defiance of the royal authority, Home of Wedderburn assailed and murdered the warden, cut off his head, knitted it to the saddle-bow by the long locks, and after-

wards exposed it upon the battlements of Home Castle.   The issue of
this experiment was not therefore such as to recommend its repetition.
Accordingly, the names of the barons who for the time possessed
most influence on the Border, are usually found in the Scottish
commissions.   The Earls of Douglas almost always added this title to
the other marks of their extensive power.   The Earls of Angus frequently exercised the authority of warden of one or other division of
the marches, and could often excite mutiny and disorder when the
rival house of Arran, or any other, was intruded into an office which
they held peculiarly their own right.   At a later period, the Earls of
Home, or Lords of Cessford, were usually wardens of the east
march ; Earls of Bothwell, or the Lords of Buccleuch and Fairni-
herst, of the middle, which usually, though not uniformly comprehended the separate office of keeper of Liddesdale ; and the rival
families of Maxwell and Johnstone, or the Lords Herries, were
wardens of the west march.   Yet even when the truncheon of warden
was consigned to a baron of extensive power and following on the
frontiers, he seems to have thought that the royal commission added
to his own natural authority, was insufficient to overawe the turbulent Borderers, and bonds of alliance and submission were, in
many cases, procured from the principal chiefs, agreeing to respect
and enforce the royal authority in the person of the warden ;* an
expedient which only serves to prove how feeble was the influence

---

* See a copy of such a bond, granted by Buccleugh and other barons, in support of
the authority of Fairnihirst as warden of the middle marches, Appendix, No. VII.   Also
a complaint of Fairnihirst to the queen against certain persons of the clan of Turnbull,
who, in breach of a similar engagement, had assaulted and wounded his men.   The mode
of redress in such cases was by procedure before the lords of the privy-council.

of the crown, and which implied in it this evil, that the chiefs who thus voluntarily agreed to support the imperfect authority of the warden, expected that it should not be over strictly exerted against those under their immediate protection. Neither was it less precarious than impolitic; for such bonds were, among men of a fiery and jealous disposition, apt to be broken through on the slightest occasion.

It was another, and yet more dangerous consequence of lodging the office of warden in the hands of the Border chieftains, that they appear, without any scruple, to have employed it less for the preservation of the public peace, than for inflicting vengeance upon their own private enemies. If the warden was engaged in deadly feud or private war with the chief of another name, he failed not to display against him the royal banner, and to proceed against him as a rebel to the crown, a conduct for which pretexts were seldom wanting. Thus, in the year 1593, Lord Maxwell, then warden of the west marches, assembled the whole strength of that part of the Border, marched against the Lord of Johnstone, and entered Annandale, with displayed banner as the king's lieutenant, with the purpose of utterly erasing and ruining that clan, which had so long rivalled his own in courage and enterprise, if not in numbers and power. The Johnstones, by the assistance of their allies the Scotts, and other friendly clans, gave the Maxwells a severe defeat, in which the warden was struck from his horse, mutilated of his hand, and then slain. And although the king took it hardly, according to Spottiswoode, that his warden, a nobleman bearing his authority, should be thus cut off, yet he found himself unable, in the circumstances of the country, to exact any vengeance for the insult. This is a remarkable

m

instance, among many, of the warden's using the royal name to serve his own private purpose, and of the slight respect in which his authority was held upon such occasions.

The Scottish wardens were allowed by the crown forage and provisions for their retinue, which consisted of a guard of horsemen, by whom they were constantly attended; these were levied from the royal domains on the Borders. They had also a proportion of the " unlaws," or fines and forfeits imposed in their warden courts, and, no doubt, had other modes of converting their authority to their own advantage, besides the opportunities their situation afforded them of extending their power and influence. The abodes of the Scottish wardens were generally their own castles on the frontiers, such as we have described them to be; and the large trees, which are still to be seen in the neighbourhood of these baronial strong-holds, served for the ready execution of justice or revenge on such malefactors as they chose to doom to death. There is, or was, a very large ash-tree near the ruins of Cessford Castle, said, by tradition, to have been often used for this purpose.

Until the English monarchy acquired some degree of power and consistency, the northern nobles usually, as in the sister country, extorted from the crown the office of wardenry, which was then held by the potent Earls of Northumberland and Westmoreland, the Lords Clifford, Dacre, and other chiefs of power on the Border. But from the reign of Henry VIII. downward, and more especially after most of the great Northumbrian families were destroyed in the great northern insurrection of 1569-70, a different line of policy was observed. Instead of conferring commissions of wardenry on the great Border families, whose wealth, extensive influence, and remote situation, already rendered them but too independent of the crown, those offices were bestowed upon men of political and military skill, such as Sir Ralph Sadler, Sir James Crofts, Sir Robert Carey, and others, the immediate dependants of the sovereign himself, who, supported by liberal allowances from the treasury, and by considerable bodies of regular troops,* were not afraid, if the discharge of their office called for it, to give offence even to the most powerful of the provincial nobility.†

For their residence, the warden of the east marches appears often to have resided at Alnwick, although Norham Castle, once belonging to the Bishops of Durham, afterwards to the crown, is recommended both by Lord Wharton and Sir Ralph Sadler ‡ as the fittest place for his abode. But the office of warden of the east marches being frequently united with the government of Berwick, that most important frontier town was often the warden's place of abode. Upon the middle marches, the Castle of Harbottell, originally the seat of the Umfravilles, and afterwards, by marriage, that of the Tailbois, being vested in the crown by forfeiture, was judged a commodious and suitable residence for the warden. The government of Carlisle being

---

* From a memorial concerning Border service, in the papers of Sir Ralph Sadler, it appears that the allowance of the captain-general of Berwick was twenty shillings per day, and the pay of the captains, soldiers, and others of the garrison in ordinary amounted to £2,400; and when extraordinary forces were stationed there, to more than twice that sum. The warden of the east marches, with his personal attendance of fifteen gentlemen, was allowed £16 : 16 : 8 for his weekly charges, and all allowances to inferior officers were upon the same scale.—SADLER's *State Papers*, Vol. II. p. 276.

† See Sadler's State Papers, Vol. II. p. 97, concerning disputes betwixt him and the Earl of Northumberland.

‡ See Border Laws, p. 344, and Sadler, Vol. II. p. 283.

usually combined with the wardenry of the western marches of England, the strong castle of that town furnished the warden with a suitable residence. Lord Scroope of Bolton, who held both these important offices long, resided there, and made considerable additions to the fortifications without, and accommodations within the castle. But Lord William Howard occupied his baronial castle of Naworth when he had the same commissions.

To ensure a general superintendance of these important offices, a lord-warden-general was sometimes nominated; but this office became less necessary, because, in time of war, there was usually a lieutenant appointed for the management of all military affairs, and during peace the general affairs of the Borders fell under the cognizance of the Lord President of the Council of the North.

The wardens had under them deputy-wardens, and warden-serjeants (popularly called land-serjeants) upon whose address and activity the quiet of the country much depended. The captains of the various royal garrisons also received orders from them; and the keeper of Tynedale, an unruly district, which required a coercive magistracy of its own, was under the command of the warden of the middle marches.

The duties committed to the charge of the wardens were of a two-fold nature, as they regarded the maintenance of law and good order amongst the inhabitants of their jurisdiction themselves, and as they concerned the exterior relations betwixt them and the opposite frontier.

In the first capacity, besides their power of controul and ministerial administration, both as head-stewards of all the crown tenements and manors within their jurisdiction, and as intromitting

with all fines and penalties, their judicial authority was very extensive. They held courts for punishment of high-treason and felony,
which the English Border laws classed under the following heads :—
I. The aiding and abetting any Scottishman, by communing, appointment, or otherwise, to rob, burn, or steal, within the realm of England.
II. The accompanying, personally, any Scottishman, while perpe-
trating such offences. III. The harbouring, concealing, or affording
guidance and protection to him after the fact. IV. The supplying
Scottishmen with arms and artillery, as jacks, splents, brigantines,
coats of plate, bills, halberds, battle-axes, bows and arrows, spears,
darts, guns, as serpentines, half-haggs, harquibusses, currys, culli-
vers, hand-guns, or daggers, without special license of the lord-
warden. V. The selling of bread and corn of any kind, or of dressed
leather, iron, or other appurtenances belonging to armour, without
special license. VI. The selling of horses, mares, nags, or geldings,
to Scottishmen, without license as aforesaid. VII. The breach of
truce, by killing or assaulting subjects and liege-men of Scotland.
VIII. The assaulting any Scottishman having a regular pass or safe-
conduct. IX. In time of war the giving tidings to the Scottish of
any exploit intended against them by the warden or his officers.
X. The conveying coined money, silver or gold, also plate or
bullion, into Scotland, above the value of forty shillings at one time.
XI. The betraying, (in time of war) the counsel of any other
Englishman tending to the annoyance of Scotland, in malice to the
party, and for his own private advantage. XII. The forging the coin
of the realm. XIII. The making appointment and holding communication with Scotchmen, or intermarrying with a Scottish woman,
without licence of the wardens, and the raising no fray against them

as in duty bound. XIV. The receiving of Scottish pilgrims with their property without license of the wardens. XV. The failing to keep the watches appointed for defence of the country. XVI. The neglecting to raise in arms to the fray, or alarm raised by the wardens or watches upon the approach of public danger. XVII. The receiving and harbouring Scottish fugitives exiled from their own country for midemeanours. XVIII. The having falsely and unjustly *fould* (*i. e.* found true and relevant) the bill of any Scotchman against an Englishman, or the having borne false witness on such matters. XIX. The having interrupted or stopped any Englishman pursuing for recovering of his stolen goods. XX. The dismissing any Scottish offender taken red-hand (*i. e.* in the manner) without special license of the lord-warden. XXI. The paying of black-mail, or protection money, whether to English or Scottish man.

All these were points of indictment in the warden courts; and the number and nature of the prohibitions they imply shew the anxiety of the English government to prevent all intercourse, as far as possible, between the natives of the two kingdoms. Most of these offences, if not all, amounted to march-treason. The accused persons were tried by a jury, and, if found guilty, suffered death by decapitation; but with the marauders of either country, the wardens used much less ceremony, and hanged them frequently, and in great numbers, without any process of law whatsoever. This was a very ordinary consummation, if we can believe a story told of Lord William Howard of Naworth. While busied deeply with his studies, he was suddenly disturbed by an officer who came to ask his commands concerning the disposal of several moss-troopers who had been just made prisoners. Displeased at the interruption, the warden answered heedlessly and angrily, " Hang them, in the devil's name;" but, when he laid aside his book, his surprise was not little, and his regret considerable, to find that his orders had been literally fulfilled.

The Scottish wardens do not appear to have held warden-courts, doubtless, because the territorial jurisdictions of sheriffdoms, stewart-ries, baillaries, and so forth, which belonged to the great families by hereditary right, and the privileges of which they jealously watched, would have been narrowed by their doing so. Besides, the Scottish hereditary judges possessed the dangerous and inconvenient power of *repledging*, as their law terms it, that is, reclaiming any accused person from courts of a co-ordinate jurisdiction, to try him by their feudal authority. It is true, the judge exercising this privilege was obliged to give security for doing justice in the premises himself; but whether his object was that of acquittal, or condemnation, his situation gave him easy means of accomplishing either without much risk of challenge. But if the Scottish wardens were more slow to hold formal courts than the English, they were not behind them in the summary execution of those offenders whom they seized upon. The ordinary proverb of Jedburgh Justice, where men were said to be hanged first and tried afterwards, appears to have taken its rise from these hasty proceedings.*

The pleasure of hunting these outlaws to their fastnesses was, to

---

* There is a similar English proverb concerning Lydford :—

> I oft have heard of Lydford law,
> Where in the morn men hang and draw,
> And sit in judgment after.
>
> BROWN's *Poems.*

some of the warlike barons who held the office of warden, its own best reward. Godscroft says, it was so peculiarly suited to the disposition of Archibald, the IXth Earl of Angus, that it might be called his proper element. He used to profess that he had as much delight in hunting a thief as others in chasing a hare; and that it was as natural to him as any other pastime or exercise was to another man. Yet the chase of this Border Nimrod (whose game was man) was by no means uniformly successful; and he was foiled on many occasions by the impracticability of the country, and the cunning of the outlaws who harboured in it.*

* " He made only one road against the outlawed thieues of the name of Armestrang. (most of them) after the king was gone home, who had been present at the casting down of their houses. He pursued them into the Tarrass Moss, which was one of their greatest strengths, and whither no host or companies had ever been known to have followed them before, and in which they did confide much, because of the straightness of the ground. He used great diligence and sufficient industry, but the success was not answerable either to his desire or other men's expectation. Neither did he forget to keep his intention close and secret, acquainting none of the people of that country therewithall, until he was ready to march. Then directing one Jordan, of Applegirth, to go to the other side, whither he knew they behoved to flee, he sent with him one of his especiall followers, whom he knew to be well affected to the service, to see that he did his duty. He himself, with the army, came openly and directly to the place of their abode, that they, fleeing from him, might fall into the hands of Applegirth, and his companie, who were come in sufficient good time, before the army could be seen to that passage which they were sent to keep. But the birds were all flown, and there was nothing left but the empty nest, having (no question) had some inkling and intelligence hereof; but it could not be tried by whom the notice had been given them. In the retreat they shew themselves, and rode about to intercept and catch such as might happen incircumspectly to straggle from the army; and they failed very narrowly to have attrapped William Douglas of Ively, a young gentleman of my lord's family, for which incircumspection he was soundly chide by him, as having thereby hazarded his own person, and his lord's honour."—GODSCROFT's History of the House of Douglas, folio, Edin. p. 430.

The Border marauders had every motive to exert their faculties for the purpose of escape; for, once seized upon, their doom was sharp and short. The mode of punishment was either by hanging or drowning.* The next tree, or the deepest pool of the nearest stream, was indifferently used on these occasions. Many moss-troopers are said to have been drowned in a deep eddy of the Jed near Jedburgh. And, in fine, the little ceremony used on these occasions added another feature to the reckless and careless character of the Borderers, who were thus accustomed to part with life with as little form as civilized men change their garments.

The wardens had it also in their power to determine many civil questions concerning the right of property violently usurped by oppression, or recovered from the hands of marauders. The mode of application seems to have been by petition. Thus, the complaint of Isabel Wetherel to Sadler, when warden of the middle marches, sets forth, that she had been found entitled to possession of a certain tenement in Bassenden, by order of the Earl of Northumberland, the former warden, and that the bailiff of the liberty still refused to execute the warrant in her favour. Another " poor oratrix," the Widow Fenwick, states in her supplication, that besides certain persons for-

---

* Drowning is a very old mode of punishment in Scotland; and in Galloway there were pits of great depth appropriated to that punishment, still called murder holes, out of which human bones have occasionally been taken in great quantities. This points out the proper interpretation of the right of pit and gallows, (in law Latin, *fossa et furca*) which has, less probably, been supposed the right of imprisoning in the pit or dungeon, and that of hanging. But the meanest baron possessed the right of imprisonment. The real meaning is, the right of inflicting death either by hanging or drowning.

merly named, she now charges some of her neighbours of the town of Wooler, whom before she had been afraid to accuse, with stealing her three cows, and prays relief in the premises. Again, John of Gilrie states, that he had made a bargain with William Archer for twenty bolls of barley, at a certain price; that Archer had only delivered ten of the said bolls, and had arrested the petitioner's horses in payment thereof, instead of implementing his bargain by delivery of the remainder. All these petitions pray for letters of charge to be directed by the warden against the parties complained upon, for answer or redress. They serve to show the complicated and mixed nature of the warden's jurisdiction, which thus seems to have admitted civil suits of a very trifling kind.

But the principal part of the warden's duty respected his transactions in the opposite kingdom in the time both of war and peace. During the time of war, he was captain-general within his wardenry, with full power to call out musters of all the fencible men betwixt the age of sixteen and sixty, duly armed and mounted according to their rank and condition, for defending the territory, or, if necessary, for invading that of the enemy. He directed, or led in person, all hostile enterprizes against the enemy's country; and it was his duty, upon such occasions, to cause to be observed the ancient rules and customs of the marches, which may be thus summed up.

I. Intercourse with the enemy was prohibited. II. He who left his company during the time of the expedition was liable to the punishment of a traitor. III. It was appointed that all should alight and fight on foot, except those commanded by the general to act as cavalry; he who remained on horseback, without such orders, forfeited his spoil and prisoners, two parts to the king, and one to the general. IV. No man was to disturb those appointed to array the host. V. If a soldier followed the chase on a horse belonging to his comrade, the owner of the horse enjoyed half the booty; and if he fled upon such horse, it was to be delivered to the sheriff as a waif on his return home, under pain of treason. VI. He that left the host after victory, though for the purpose of securing his prisoner, lost his ransom. If any one slew another's prisoner he was liable to pay his ransom; or, in failure of his ability to do so, was sentenced to death. In general, it was found to be the use of the Marches that every man might take as many prisoners as he could secure, exchanging tokens with them that they might afterwards know each other. VII. Any one accused of seizing his comrade's prisoner was obliged to find security in the hands of the warden serjeant. Disputed prisoners were to be placed in the hands of the warden; and the party found ultimately wrong to be amerced in a fine of ten pounds. VIII. Relates to the evidence in the case of such dispute. He who could bring his own countrymen in evidence, of whatsoever quality, was preferred as the true captor; failing of this mode of proof, recourse was had to the prisoner's oath. IX. No prisoner of such rank as to lead an hundred men was either to be dismissed upon security or ransomed, for the space of fifteen days, without leave of the warden. X. He who dismounted a prisoner was entitled to half of his ransom. XI. Whosoever detected a traitor was entitled to the reward of one hundred shillings; whoever aided his escape, suffered the pain of death. XII. Relates to the firing of the beacons in Scotland; the stewards of Annandale and Kirkcudbright were liable in the fine of one merk for each default in that matter. XIII. He who did not join the array of the country upon the signal

of the beacon-lights, or who left it during the continuance of the
English invasion without lawful excuse, his goods were forfeited,
and his person placed at the warden's will. XIV. In case of any
Englishman being taken within Scotland, he was not suffered to depart
under any safe conduct save that of the king or warden; and a
similar protection was necessary to enable him to return and treat of
his ransom. If this was neglected, he became the prisoner of whatever Scotchman happened to seize him. XV. Any Scottishman
dismissing his prisoner, when a host was collected either to enter
England or defend against invasion was punished as a traitor. XVI.
In the partition of spoil, two portions were allowed to each bowman.
XVII. Whoever deserted his commander and comrades, and abode
not in the field to the uttermost, his goods were forfeited, and his
person liable to the punishment of a traitor. XVIII. Whoever bereft
his comrade of horse, spoil, or prisoner, was liable in the pains of
treason, if he did not make restitution after the right of property
became known to him.

These military regulations were arranged by William Earl of
Douglas, by the advice of the most experienced marchmen, in the
year 1468.* But it appears that they were adopted by the English

* The exordium of these regulations is remarkable. It runs thus :—" Be it remembered, that on the 18th day of December, 1468, Earl William Douglas assembled the
whole lords, freeholders, and eldest Borderers that best knowledge had, at the College of
Linclouden, and there he caused those lords and Borderers bodily to be sworn, the
holy Gospel touched, that they justly and truly, after their cunning, should decrete, de-
cern, deliver, and put in order and writing, the statutes, ordinances, and uses of marche
that were ordained in Black Archibald of Douglas' days, and Archibald his son's days,
in time of warfare ; and they came again to him advisedly with these statutes and ordinances which were in time of warfare before. The said Earl William seeing the sta-

with the necessary alterations, for a copy of them is found in the Manuscript of Mr. Bell, the accurate and laborious warden-clerk of the western marches of England, in the reign of Queen Elizabeth. At least, they are so well suited to the genius of the country and age, that there can be no doubt that they express the general spirit of the military enactments on both sides of the Border.

We must not omit to state, that as the wardens of the marches had it in charge to conduct the war between the countries, so they had also power of concluding truces with the opposite warden for their own jurisdictions. Such an indenture entered into between " the noble lords and mighty," Henry Percy, Earl of Northumberland, and Archibald Douglas, Lord of Galloway, at the water of Esk, beside Solway, on the 15th March, 1323-4, not only concludes a truce between their bounds on each side, but declares, "That if any great power of either country shall prepare to invade the other, each of the said lords shall do what they can to hinder it; and if they cannot prevent it, they shall give the other party fifteen days notice, and shall themselves abstain from riding with the host, and shall do all in their power, without fraud or guile, to keep the aggressors out of their bounds. Intimation of the rupture of the truce was to be given by a certain term, at the Chapel of Salom, or Solway. All

tutes in writing decreed and delivered by the said lords and Borderers thought them right speedful and profitable to the Borderers; the which statutes, ordinances, and points of warfare he took, and the whole lords and Borderers he caused bodily to be sworn that they should maintain and supply him at their goodly power, to do the law, upon those that should break the statutes underwritten. Also the said Earl William, and lords and eldest Borderers, made certain points to be treason in time of warfare to be used, which were no treason before his time, but to be treason in his time, and in all time coming."

prisoners on either side were to be freely delivered. If any single freebooter committed theft in breach of the covenant, he was to be hanged or beheaded ; if a company were concerned in the delict, one should be put to death, and the others amerced in double the value of their spoil." This indenture rather resembles a treaty between two independent princes, than an agreement between the crown officers of the west marches of England and Scotland. Something, doubtless, is to be ascribed to the great power of the Percy and the Douglas, who could, unquestionably, make their authority go much farther than chieftains of less weight could have done, though holding the same ostensible commission. Still, however, the powers of the wardens in waging war, or concluding truces, were of an extensive and unlimited nature.

In time of peace, the warden had the more delicate task of at the same time maintaining the amicable relations betwixt the two countries, and of preventing or retaliating the various grievances and encroachments committed by the Borderers of the opposite kingdom upon the frontiers under his rule.

The most constant and almost unremitted subject of complaint, was the continual incursions of the moss-troopers upon both sides. This species of injury early required the redress of inter-national laws or customs. For example, although the right of the native of the invaded country to protect his property against the robber could not be denied, and although it was equally his inherent privilege to pursue the marauders with such force as he could assemble, and recover the plunder if he could overtake them within the bounds of the kingdom which they had invaded, yet it was a question of national law, how far he was entitled to continue pursuit in an hostile manner into the territory of the sister country, and there to recover his property by force. At the same time, it was not to be expected that the intervention of a small river, or of an imaginary line, should be a protection for the robbers and their booty, against the just resentment of the party injured, while in the very act of hot pursuit. The Border Laws, therefore, allowed the party plundered not only to follow his goods upon the spur, and enter the opposite kingdom for recovery thereof, without licence or safe conduct, but even to do the like, at any time within six days after his sustaining the injury, providing always he went straight to some honest man of good fame inhabiting the Marches which he had thus entered, and declared to him the cause of his coming, inviting him to attend him and witness his conduct. The wardens of either realm, or those duly authorised by them, were entitled to pursue fugitives or offenders into the precincts of the neighbouring realm, by what was called the *hot-trod*. This pursuit was maintained with a lighted piece of turf carried on a spear, with hue and cry, bugle-horn, and blood-hound, that all might be aware of the purpose of the party. If any native of the country thus entered intercepted the party or their blood-hound in such *hot-trod*, he was liable to be billed, or indicted at the next day of truce, and delivered up to the warden whom he had offended. It was, however, recommended to the pursuers of the *hot-trod* to stop at the nearest town of the realm whose frontiers they had thus passed, and give declaration of the purpose of the chase, and require the inhabitants to go along to witness his procedure. If the pursuers did unlawful damage within the opposite realm, they were liable to be delivered to the warden thereof for condign punishment.

But these provisions were only calculated to remedy such evils as befel *de recenti*, since to have sought reparation at their own hand and by their own strength for such as were of older date, would have made the Borders a constant scene of uproar, retaliation, and bloodshed. Some course of justice, therefore, was to be fallen upon, by which justice might be done to those who had sustained wrong from the depredators of the opposite country, by means more regular and less hazardous than the ready measures of forcible retaliation.

The first regulations laid down on this subject were conformable to the ideas of that military age, which referred all matters difficult of instant proof, to the judgment of God in single combat. Eleven knights of Northumberland, and as many of the Scottish east marches, with the Sheriff of Northumberland on the one side, and of Roxburgh and Berwick on the other, met in the 33d of Henry III. anno 1249. These martial formalists made some regulations for recovery of debts due by those of the one kingdom to the other, and for the re-delivery of fugitive bondsmen.* But they unanimously declared that every Scottishman accused of having committed any crime in England, of which he could offer to purge himself by the combat, could only be summoned to answer at fixed places on the marches. Also that all persons, of whatever rank or degree, dwelling between Totness in Cornwall, and Caithness in Scotland, might be appealed to battle on the marches, excepting only the sovereign, and the Bishops of St. Andrews and Dunkeld.† Goods alleged to be

---

* It is the Scottish copy of indenture which exists. That of England must have been *mutatis mutandis*.

† Churchmen of corresponding dignity in England must have been unquestionably admitted to the same privilege.

stolen from England might be sued for by the owner in the court of
the Scottish lord within whose bounds they were discovered; but if
the accused party denied the charge, there was no other alternative
but the combat.   Yet, if the accused did not feel bold in his innocence,
or determined in his denial, he might quit himself of the charge,
without the risk of combat, in the following singular manner.   He
was to bring the stolen ox, horse, cow, or other animal, to the brink
of the river Tweed or Eske, where they form the frontier line, and
drive it into the stream.   If the animal escaped alive to the other
kingdom, he had no further trouble in the matter; but if it was
drowned before it reached the middle stream, then he was condemned
liable to the plaintiff for its estimable value.   Lastly, these experienced men of war decreed, by a sweeping clause, that no inhabitant
of either kingdom could prove his property in any goods actually
possessed by an inhabitant of the other, unless by the *body of a
man*, that is, by entering the lists either personally, or by a delegated
champion.

Every dispute between the inhabitants, on either side, was therefore decided by personal duel, and even churchmen were bound to
combat by proxy.   The clergy of England numbered this among
the grievances which they reported to the legate Otho, in the year
1237.   They state, that by an abuse of a mandate of the kings of
England and Scotand, not only simple clerks, but even abbots and
priors within the diocese of Carlisle, were, on the challenge of any
one of the kingdom of Scotland, compelled to undertake, with lance
and sword, and otherwise armed, the combat, which was called *aera*,*

---

* *Aera*, or *aerea*, a word of uncertain meaning; and, so far as I know, only occurring

o

to be fought on the frontiers of the two kingdoms ; so that the abbot
or prior, of whatsoever order, was obliged to have a champion, and,
in case of his defeat, was subjected to the penalty of one overcome in
the appeal to God, as in our own time, continues the remonstrance,
was experienced by the Prior of Lideley.*

When priests were not excused, the combats among the laity
must have been very numerous.   But in later times, the appeal to
combat was less universally admitted, and the state of confusion and
depredation on the Borders increasing, as we have observed, after the
usurpation of Scotland by Edward I., rendered it necessary to seek
for other modes of checking theft than that by which the true man
was compelled to expose his life in combat with the robber.   It
became, therefore, a principal part of the warden's duty, when that
duty was conscientiously performed, during the time of peace, to
maintain a regular and friendly intercourse with those on the
opposite side, both for preventing and punishing all disorders committed by the lawless on either territory.   But besides these communications, it was a principal point of their commission, that the wardens
on either side should hold days of truce, or of march, as frequently as
could be made convenient, in which, with great solemnity, they
enquired into and remedied the offences complained of by the
subjects of either realm.

The wardens, on these occasions, took the field attended by the

---

in this sense in the present passage.   It may allude to the area or inclosed space within
which the combatants fought.   *Aerea*, and *area*, are explained by Du Cange and in the
supplement, as synonimous, and as meaning an inclosed space, neither cultivated nor
ploughed.   The circular inclosure near Penrith, called King Arthur's Round Table, was
probably an area of this kind.

  * *Annales Burtonenses*, apud Gale, vol. I. p. 292.

lords, knights, esquires, and men of name within their jurisdictions, all in their best arms, and well mounted. The two troops paused on the frontiers of both kingdoms, until they had exchanged assurance for observing and keeping the peace from sunrise to sunset. The two wardens then met in great form, mutually embraced each other, and, surrounded by those of the best rank in their Marches, they proceeded to examine the *bills*, or complaints tendered on either side. If the persons accused were judged guilty, the bills were said to be *filed*, or *fouled ;* if the complaint was dismissed, the bill was said to be *cleansed*. Where doubt occurred, the question of cleansing or fouling a bill was tried either by the honour of the wardens, or by a jury of six English and six Scottish gentlemen,† mutually chosen, or by a vower-public, that is, a referee belonging to the country of the party accused, and mutually chosen by the plaintiff and the defendant. In some cases the accused was permitted to exculpate himself by oath, which, terrible as its denunciations were, did not always prevent perjury.‡ In like manner, the plaintiff, or party who

---

* See the form of a bill fouled on William Hall, an English Borderer, at a warden meeting between the Earl of Northumberland, the Earl of Bothwell, and Lord of Cesford, 10th October, 1559, Appendix, No. VIII.

† The jurors took the following oath: " You shall clean no bills worthy to be fouled, you shall foul no bills worthy to be cleaned, but shall do that what appeareth with truth, for the maintenance of the peace, and suppressing of attempts. So help you God."— *M. S. of* Mr. BELL, *Warden Clerk, quoted in Introduction to* NICHOLSON's *History of Cumberland and Westmoreland.*

‡ The following were the terms of this oath for excusing a bill, as it was termed:— " You shall swear by heaven above you, hell beneath you, by your part of paradise, by all that God made in six days and seven nights, and by God himself, you are whart out sackless of art, part, way, witting, ridd, kenning, having, or recetting of any of the goods and cattels named in this bill. So help you God."—BELL's *Manuscript, as above.*

preferred the bill, was bound to make oath to the estimated value of his goods.* Perjury, in such cases, was punished by imprisonment and infamy; and if the plaintiff over-rated the goods he had lost, the amount might be taxed by a jury of both nations.

With respect to the offenders against whom bills were presented, it was the duty of the warden to have them in custody, in readiness for their answer; and in case the bills were fouled, he was bound to deliver them up to the opposite warden, by whom they were imprisoned until they had paid a *single and two doubles*, that is to say, treble the value of the estimated goods in the bill. To produce these offenders was generally the most difficult part of the warden's duty. He could not keep them in confinement until the day of truce; for, independently that they were sometimes persons of power and rank, their numbers were too great to be detained in custody. The wardens, therefore, usually took bonds from the chief, kinsmen, or allies of the accused party, binding him or them to enter him prisoner within the iron gate of the warden's castle, or else to make him forthcoming when called for.† He against whom a bill was thrice fouled, was liable to the penalty of death. If the offender endeavoured to rescue himself after being lawfully delivered over to the opposite warden, he was liable to the punishment of death, or otherwise, at the warden's pleasure, as being guilty of a breach of the assurance.

---

* The oath of estimation was as follows: "You shall leile price make, and trueth say, what your goods were worth at the time of their taking, to have been bought and sold in a market all at one time, and that you know no other recovery but this. So help you God."—*Ibid.*

† See such an obligation, Appendix, No. IX.

The extent of the mutual damage sustained by both kingdoms being thus ascertained, a list, in the form of an account-current, was made up by enumerating all the bills fouled on each side, and the value was summed by striking a balance against the country whose depredators had been most active.* It seems probable the extremity of the legal satisfaction was seldom exacted or obtained. The resentment of the depredators and of their kinsmen was dreaded; the common usage took away the natural abhorrence of the crime; plunder was a privilege which each party assumed in their turn; and as it often happened that the same person against whom a bill was fouled for one fact, had himself been a sufferer, and was a plaintiff in a charge preferred against others,† it is probable that some extra-judicial settlement often took the matter out of the warden court. Nay, it frequently happened, when enormities had gone to great extent during any particular time of misrule, that a veil was dropped over the past, and satisfaction exacted from neither party. At other times, when the crowns were determined strictly to maintain the relations of amity with each other, the course of justice was more severely enforced. Men of high rank, the chiefs of clans, and others, responsible, by their situation and authority, for the conduct of those under them, were sometimes delivered up to be kept in ward in the opposite kingdom until the misdeeds of their deputies and

---

* See such an account-current in the Appendix, No. X.

† For example, in the List of Attempts, No. X. of the Appendix, several bills are fouled on the Laird of Mangertoun, chief of the Armstrongs; and he, in return, obtains several bills to be fouled upon English Borderers for similar devastations.

Hanc veniam damus petimusque vicissim.

dependents were atoned for by payment of the valuation and fines.
But it does not appear that the wardens could proceed to attach
these persons on their simple authority. Their delivery seems to
have followed in consequence of an agreement to that purpose, by
special commissioners, vested with full powers from both crowns.
To such commissioners also belonged the power of making new laws
and enactments on the Border, the wardens being limited by the
existing rules of march.

Besides depredations by robbery on each side, the wardens, at
their days of truce, were wont to demand and receive satisfaction
for other encroachments, such as sowing or pasturing by the natives
of one kingdom within the territories of the other, offences subject to
be fouled by bill, and punished by mulct, and the more frequent
invasion for the purpose of cutting wood in the forests of the opposite
frontier, or hunting, hawking, and disporting in the same without
license asked or received. These encroachments, which will remind
the reader of Chevy Chace, often gave rise to scuffles, and even to
bloodshed.*

---

* Such an event was prevented by the prudence of Sir **Robert Carey**. " The next
summer after, I fell into a cumbersome trouble, but it was not in the nature of thieves
or malefactors. There had been an ancient custom of the Borderers, when they were
at quiet, for the opposite Border to send to the warden of the middle march to desire
leave that they might come into the Borders of England and hunt with their greyhounds
for deer towards the end of summer, which was never denied them. But towards the
end of Sir John Foster's government, when he grew very old and weak, they took bold-
ness on them, and without leave asking, would come into England, and hunt at their
pleasure, and stay their own time ; and when they were a-hunting, their servants would
come with carts, and cut down as much wood as every one thought would serve his turn,
and carry it away to their houses in Scotland. Sir John's imbecility and weakness occasioned them to continue this misdemeanour some four or five years together, before he

When the business of the meeting was over, the wardens retired, after taking a courteous leave of each other ; and it was a custom of

---

left his office. And after my Lord Euers had the office, he was so vexed and troubled with the disorders of the country, as all the time he remained there, he had no leisure to think of so small a business, and to redress it ; so that now they began to hold it lawful to come and go at their pleasures without leave asking. The first summer I entered, they did the like. The Armstrongs kept me so on work that I had no time to redress it ; but having over-mastered them, and the whole march being brought to a good stay and quietness, the beginning of next summer I wrote to Ferniherst, the warden over against me, to desire him to acquaint the gentlemen of his march, that I was no way unwilling to hinder them of their accustomed sports to hunt in England as they ever had done, but withal I would not by my default dishonour the queen and myself, to give them more liberty than was fitting. I prayed him, therefore, to let them know, that if they would, according to the ancient custom, send to me for leave, they should have all the content-ment I could give them ; if otherwise they would continue their wonted course, I would do my best to hinder them.

"Notwithstanding this letter, within a month after, they came and hunted as they used to do without leave, and cut down wood, and carried it away. I wrote again to the warden, and plainly told him, I would not suffer one other affront, but if they came again without leave they should dearly aby* it. For all this they would not be warned : but towards the end of the summer they came again to their wonted sports. I had taken order to have present word brought me, which was done. I sent my two deputies with all the speed they could make, and they took along with them such gentlemen as were in their way, with my forty horse, and about one of the clock they came up to them, and set upon them ; some hurt was done; but I gave especial orders they should do as little hurt, and shed as little blood, as possibly they could. They observed my command, only they broke all their carts, and took a dozen of the principal gentlemen that were there, and brought them to me at Withrington, where I then lay. I made them welcome, and gave them the best entertainment that I could. They lay in the castle two or three days, and so I sent them home, they assuring me, that they never would hunt there again without leave, which they did truly perform all the time I stayed there ; and I many times met them myself, and hunted with them two or three days ; and so we continued good neighbours ever after : but the king complained to the queen very grievously of this fact. The queen and council liked very well of what I had done ; but, to give the king some satisfaction to content him, my two officers were commanded to the Bishop of

* Suffer for it.

the march, that, before dismissing the gentlemen who attended them, each warden demanded of the most respectable and experienced Borderers, their opinion of the business of the day, and requested them to say whether the rules of the march had been observed, and justice equally distributed.

When these days of march-truce were held regularly, and justice punctually administered, the Borders were comparatively but little disturbed; and the wardens on both sides were usually instructed, from their several courts, not to insist too particularly on points of mere form or of difficult discussion, but to leave them for discussion by special commissioners.

But although these regulations were perhaps as wise as the case admitted, yet the union of the opposite wardens, so necessary to preserve the peace of the frontier, was always of precarious duration. They were soldiers by profession, of hostile countries, jealous at once of their own honour and that of their nation, surrounded by warlike partizans and dependants, who animated every disagreement into a quarrel, and must therefore, on the whole, have preferred taking satisfaction for any insult at their own hand, and by their own force, than seeking it in a more peaceful manner from the opposite warden.

Sir Robert Cary gives us a singular picture of their conduct towards each other. Being deputy-warden of the east marches, he sent to Sir Robert Kerr of Cessford, the opposite Scottish warden, to ap-

---

Durham's, there to remain prisoners during her majesty's pleasure. Within a fortnight I had them out again, and there was no more of this business. The rest of the time I stayed there, it was governed with great quietness."—CAREY's *Memoirs*. Edit. 1803, p. 110.

point a meeting for regulation of the Border affairs. But Cessford apparently wished to anticipate one part of the affairs to be discussed. Having therefore received Carey's messenger, filled him with drink and put him to bed, he mounted his horse, entered England with an armed attendance, seized a Borderer against whom he alleged some cause of quarrel, and put him to death at his own door. After this exploit, he delivered a civil answer to Sir Robert Carey's servant, agreeing to the proposed interview. It was now the turn of the English warden to be offended; he neglected the appointment without notice to Cessford, leaving him to wait several hours at the place of meeting. The Borderers began to stir on both sides, and raids were made out of Scotland so often as three or four times a-week. The severe measures of Sir Robert Carey, who executed all thieves taken in the manner, or red-hand as it was called, in some degree checked these inroads. At length a noted depredator, called Geordie Bourne, a special favourite of the Lord of Cessford, fell into his hands. The gentlemen of the country entreated him to enter into terms with Sir Robert Kerr for sparing this man's life; but, having visited him in disguise, and learned his habits from his own mouth, Carey resolved that no conditions should save him, and caused him to be executed accordingly before the gates of the castle.*

---

* " When all things were quiet," says Sir Robert Carey, " and the watch set at night, after supper, about ten of the clock, I took one of my men's liveries, and put it about me, and took two other of my servants with me in their liveries, and we three, as the warden's men, came to the provost-marshal's where Bourne was, and were let into his chamber. We sat down by him, and told him that we were desirous to see him, because we heard he was stout and valiant, and true to his friend, and that we were sorry our master could not be moved to save his life. He voluntarily of himself said, that he had lived long enough to do so many villanies as he had done, and withal told us, that he had lain with

P

In revenge of the death of this man, Sir Robert Kerr very nearly surprised a party of Carey's servants at Norham, who must have been cut to pieces, had they not, by their master's command, slept that night in the castle. The dissention between these two officers continued, until, upon such an occasion as we have noticed, p. cix, Cessfurd, along with the Lord of Buccleuch, was appointed to be delivered into England, when, with that sort of generous confidence which qualified the ferocity of the Border character, he chose his enemy, Sir Robert Carey, for his guardian; after which they lived on the most amicable terms with each other.*

about forty men's wives, what in England what in Scotland; and that he had killed seven Englishmen with his own hands, cruelly murdering them; that he had spent his whole time in whoring, drinking, stealing, and taking deep revenge for slight offences."—*Memoirs*, p. 73.

* Such tracts are like a glimpse of sunshine amid the lowering of a storm. Carey relates the circumstances which led to these agreements in the pithy style of Queen Elizabeth's time. " There had been commissioners in Berwick chosen by our Queen and the King of Scots, for the better quieting of the Borders. By their industry they found a great number of malefactors guilty, both in England and Scotland; and they took order that the officers of Scotland should deliver such offenders as were found guilty in their jurisdictions, to the opposite officers in England, to be detained prisoners, till they had made satisfaction for the goods they had taken out of England. The like order was taken with the wardens of England, and days prefixed for the delivery of them all. And in case any of the officers on either side should omit their dutys in not delivering the prisoners at the days and places appointed, that then there should a course be taken by the sovereigns, that what chief officer soever should offend herein, he himself should be delivered and detained, till he had made good what the commissioners had agreed upon.

" The English officers did punctually, at the day and place, deliver their prisoners, and so did most of the officers of Scotland; only the Lord Bocleugh and Sir Robert Car were faulty. They were complained of, and new days appointed for the delivery of their prisoners. Bocleugh was the first that should deliver, and he failing, entered himself prisoner into Berwick, there to remain till those officers under his charge were delivered to free him. He chose for his guardian Sir William Selby, master of the

Even the meetings of truce, appointed for the settlement of grievances betwixt the wardens, were very often converted into scenes of battle and bloodshed. Each warden, being themselves such fiery and martial characters as we have described, came to the place of meeting, attended by his guard of horsemen, and by all the warlike clans of his district, completely armed. Among these must often have been many names betwixt whom deadly feud existed; and, if

ordnance of Berwick. When Sir Robert Car's day of delivery came, he failed too, and my Lord Hume, by the king's command, was to deliver him prisoner into Berwick upon the like terms, which was performed. Sir Robert Car, contrary to all men's expectations, chose me for his guardian, and home I brought him to my own house, after he was delivered to me. I lodged him as well as I could, and took order for his diet, and men to attend on him; and sent him word, that (although by his harsh carriage towards me ever since I had that charge, he could not expect any favour, yet) hearing so much goodness of him, that he never broke his word, if he would give me his hand and credit to be a true prisoner, he should have no guard set upon him, but have free liberty for his friends in Scotland to have ingress and regress to him as oft as he pleased. He took this very kindly at my hands, accepted of my offer, and sent me thanks.

" Some four days passed; all which time his friends came unto him, and he kept his chamber. Then he sent to me and desired me I would come and speak with him, which I did; and after long discourse, charging and recharging one another with wrong and injuries, at last before our parting, we became good friends, with great protestations on his side, never to give me occasion of unkindness again. After our reconciliation, he kept his chamber no longer, but dined and supped with me. I took him abroad with me at the least thrice a week, a-hunting, and every day we grew better friends. Bocleugh, in a few days after, had his pledges delivered, and was set at liberty; but Sir Carr could not get his, so that I was commanded to carry him to York, and there to deliver him prisoner to the archbishop, which accordingly I did. At our parting, he professed great love unto me for the kind usage I had shown him, and that I should find the effects of it upon his delivery, which he hoped would be shortly.

" Thus we parted; and not long after his pledges were got and brought to York, and he set at liberty. After his return home, I found him as good as his word. We met oft at days of truce, and I had as good justice as I could desire; and so we continued very kind and good friends all the time I stayed in that march, which was not long."— CAREY's *Memoirs.* Edit. 1808, p. 80.

they had no peculiar cause of animosity, their nations were habitually hostile, and it was the interest of the Borderers to exasperate that national animosity. Add to this, that the principal depredators being present, with their friends and allies, they had every motive to instigate any brawl which could interrupt the course of justice. It was therefore, often in vain, that all men at these days of truce were discharged from *baugling* (brawling,) or reproving with the subjects of the opposite realm, or from disturbing the assurance of peace, by word, deed, or countenance. Where there were so many combustible materials, the slightest spark served to kindle a conflagration.

Accordingly, repeated instances occur of such affrays happening, in which much gentle blood, and frequently that of the wardens themselves, stained the days appointed for the administration of Border justice. Thus, in the year 1511, Sir Robert Kerr of Cessford, warden of the middle marches, while at a march-meeting, was struck through with a lance by the bastard Heron, and dispatched by Starked and Lilburn, two English Borderers; a slaughter which, amongst other causes of quarrel, gave ground to the war between England and Scotland, terminated by the fatal battle of Flodden.

On a subsequent occasion, when Sir Francis Russell, third son of the second Earl of Bedford, chanced to be slain, the Scots appear to have been aggressors in their turns. Camden gives the following account of a fray which took place in the year 1585:—

" For when Sir John Foster, and Thomas Carre of Fernihurst, wardens of the middle marches betwixt the two kingdoms of England and Scotland, had appointed a meeting on the 27th of June, about certain goods unjustly taken away, and security was given on both sides by oath, according to custom, and proclamation made,

that no man should *harm other, by word, deed, or look,* (as the Borderers speak,) the Scots came to the place of meeting armed in battle
array, with ensigns displayed, and drums beating, contrary to custom
and beyond expectation, being in number about three thousand,
whereas the English were not above three hundred. Scarce were
the wardens sat to hear the complaints, when on a sudden, upon an
Englishman's being taken pilfering, there arose a tumult, and the
Scots discharging a volley of shot, slew Russel, with some others,
put the English to flight, and eagerly pursuing them the space of
four miles into England, carried off some prisoners. Who was the
author of this slaughter was not certainly known. The English laid
the fault upon Arran, now chancellor of Scotland, and upon
Fernihurst. The queen pressed, both by her letters and commissioners, to have the murderers delivered into her hands, inasmuch as
Henry IV., King of England, had formerly delivered up into the
hands of James IV., King of Scots, William Heron and seven Englishmen, for killing Robert Carre of Cessford upon a day of meeting;
and Morton, the late regent, sent Carmichael, a Scot, into England
for killing George Heron. The king protested his own innocency in
the matter, and promised to send, not only Fernihurst immediately
into England, but the chancellor too, if they could be convicted by
clear and lawful proofs to have premeditately infringed the security, or
procured the murder. Fenwick, an Englishman, accused Fernihurst
of the fact to his face; he avoided it by a flat denial, because the
other could produce no Scottishman for a witness. For in these trials
on the Borders, according to a certain privilege and custom agreed on
amongst the Borderers, none but a Scot is to be admitted for a witness
against a Scot, and none but an Englishman against an Englishman;

insomuch, that if all the Englishmen which were upon the place
had seen the murder committed before their eyes, yet their tes-
timony had been of no value, unless some Scottishman also did
witness the same.   Nevertheless, Arran was confined to his house,
and Fernihurst was committed to custody at Dundee, where
afterwards he died: a stout and able warrior, ready for any great
attempts and undertakings, and of an immoveable fidelity to the
Queen of Scots, and the king her son; having been once or twice
turned out of all his lands and fortunes, and banished the sight of his
country and children, which yet he endured patiently, and, after so
many crosses falling upon him together, perished unshaken and
always like himself."*

One of the latest of these affrays has been described with some lively
colouring in the rude rhymes of an old Scottish minstrel.   The place
of meeting was the Reidswair, a spot on the very ridge of a bleak
and waste tract of mountains, called the Carter-fells, which divide
England from Scotland.   The Scottish clans of the middle marches
arrived in arms and in attendance upon Sir John Carmichael of
Carmichael; and, from the opposite side, the Borderers of Tynedale
and Redesdale advanced, with " jack and spear and bended bows,"
with Sir John Forster, the English warden.   Yet the meeting began
in mirth and good neighbourhood; and while the wardens proceeded
to the business of the day, the armed Borderers of either party
engaged in sports, and played at cards or dice, or loitered around the
moor.   The merchants, or pedlars, erected their temporary booths,

* Camden's Annalls at the year 1585, in Kennet's History of England, vol. II.
p. 505.

and displayed their wares, and the whole had the appearance of a peaceful holiday or rural fair. In the midst of this good humour, the wardens were observed to raise their voices in angry altercation. A bill had been *fouled* upon one Farnstein, an English Borderer, who, according to custom and law of march, ought to have been delivered up to the Scots. The excuses made by Sir John Forster did not satisfy the Scottish warden, who taxed him with partiality. At this the English warden, rising suddenly, and drawing up his person so as to have the full advantage of all his height, contemptuously desired Carmichael to match himself with his equals in birth and quality. These signs of resentment were sufficient hints to the Tynedale Borderers, who immediately shot off a flight of arrows among the Scots. The war-cry and slogan of the different clans then rose on either side; and these ready warriors, immediately starting to their weapons, fought it out manfully. By the opportune arrival of the citizens of Jedburgh, armed with fire-arms, the Scots obtained the victory; Sir George Heron of Chipchase, and some other Englishmen of rank, being slain on the spot, and Sir John Forster himself, with others of his retinue, made prisoners. This affray gave great offence to Elizabeth; and the Regent Morton, stooping before her displeasure, sent Carmichael to answer for his conduct at the court of England, where, however, he was not long detained.

Besides the duties of annoying the hostile frontiers in war, and maintaining amicable relations with them in time of peace, there was a sort of mixed obligation on the wardens, of a nature somewhat delicate; they were expected to avail themselves of their proper strength, to retaliate such offences as they could not obtain reparation for from the opposite warden, or contentedly sit down under, without compromising their own honour and that of their country. This mode of compensating injuries by retaliation always added considerably to the discords and inroads upon the Borders, and licensed for the time the enterprises of the most desperate marauders. One or two instances of the manner in which the wardens acted on such occasions, and of the circumstances which gave rise to their appearing in arms, will complete our account of the duties of these guardians of the frontiers.

The Debateable Land (before its final division) was a constant subject of dissention between the opposite wardens of the west marches. To require satisfaction from the English for the inroads of the Borderers inhabiting this tract, or to render satisfaction to them for what the people of the Debateable Land had suffered from the Scottish in return, would have been to acknowledge the district to be a part of England. Lord Maxwell, therefore, in 1550, declared his intention of marching against the men of the Debateable Land, not as Englishmen, but as Scottish rebels, and laying waste their possessions. Lord Dacre, the opposite warden, acted with equal spirit and prudence. He drew out the forces of his march upon the verge of the acknowledged possessions of England, thus affording countenance, but no active assistance, to the men of the Debateable ground. These, a fierce and untractable set of people, chiefly of the clans of Armstrong and Græme, seeing themselves well supported, *pricked* or skirmished with Lord Maxwell on his entering their district, and took one or two of his followers, by which repulse, backed, by the good countenance shewn by the English warden, the expedition of Lord Maxwell was disconcerted. This brief campaign is mentioned in King Edward IVth's Journal.*

Numerous occasions took place, when the warden, on either or both sides, resenting some real or supposed denial of justice, endeavoured to right themselves by *riding*, as it was termed, that is, making incursions on the opposite country. This was at no time more common than in the year 1596, when a singular incident gave rise to a succession of these aggressions, and well nigh occasioned a war between the kingdoms.

In the year 1596, there was a meeting on the Borders of Liddesdale betwixt the deputies of the Lord Scroope of Bolton, warden of the west marches, and the Lord of Buccleuch, keeper of Liddesdale. When the business of the day was over, and the meeting broken up, the English chanced to observe a Scottish Borderer, of the clan of Armstrong, called Willie of Kinmont, celebrated for his depredations. He had been in attendance, like other Border riders, upon the Scottish officer, and was now returning home on the north side of the river Liddle. Although he was on Scottish ground, and that the assurance of truce ought to have protected him, the temptation to seize an offender so obnoxious was too great to be resisted. A large body of English horsemen crossed the river, pursued and took him, and lodged him in Carlisle Castle. As Lord Scroope refused to give

---

* " August 16, 1549. The Earl of Maxwell came down to the North Border with a good power to overthrow the Gremes, who were a certain family that were yielded to me; but the Lord Dacre stood before his face with a good band of men, and so put him from his purpose; and the gentlemen called Gremes skirmished with the said earl, slaying certain of his men."

Kinmont up, although thus unwarrantably taken prisoner, Buccleuch resolved to set him at liberty by force, and, with a small body of determined followers, he surprised the Castle of Carlisle, and without doing any injury to the garrison, or to the warden, carried off the prisoner. This spirited action was so much admired by the Scottish nation, that even King James, however much afraid of displeasing Elizabeth, and though urged by her with the most violent complaints and threats, hesitated to deliver up the warden who had so well sustained the dignity of his office and the immunities of the kingdom. But this act of reprisal gave rise to many others. Sir Thomas Musgrave rode into Scotland, and made spoil like an ordinary Borderer ; and Henry Widdrington laid waste and burned Cavers, belonging to the Sheriff of Teviotdale. Buccleuch's life was said to be the aim of these marauders, and, as it was alleged, with the privity of the Queen of England.❋ On the other hand, the Lords of Buccleuch and Cessford vexed the English Border by constant and severe incursions, so that nothing was heard of but burning, *hership* (devastation,) and slaughter. In Tynedale, Buccleuch seized upon no less than thirty-six English freebooters, and put them to death without mercy. The wrath of Elizabeth waxed uncontroulable.† " I marvel,"

❋ Rymer's Fœdera, vol. XVI. pp. 307, 308.

† Her instructions to her ambassador, Sir William Bowes, mark at once the state of the marches and the extremity of her majesty's displeasure. They occur in Rymer's Fœdera, vol. XIV. p. 112.

" ELIZABETH R.

" Trusty and welbeloved, We greet you well.

" When you departed, we delivered you our full pleasure how you should, upon your arryval at Carlile, and how you should address yourself to the king upon his approach to the Borders, or upon any difficulties occurring in the treaties, since which time we

are her own royal expressions, " how the king thinks me so base minded as to sit down with such dishonourable treatment. Let him know we will be satisfied, or else"—— Some of James's ancestors would have bid her

Choke in thy threat. We can say or as loud.

But James judged it more safe to pacify her by surrendering his

have received from our wardens nothing but frequent advertisements, both from the east and middle marches, especially how daily they are spoyled and burned by the incursions from the opposite borders : and for more open shewe of injury, Buklugh himself, the king's officer, hath been a fresh ringleader of the same, whereby appeareth how little likelihood there is that such wardens will restrayne their inferiors, or the king himselfe reforme any thing, seing he doth not only tollerat but cherish them, since they were found most faultie, and hath, in lieu of punishment, given some of them newe favors, and left us neglected in the eye of the world, with frutelesse promises of satisfaction ; by expectation whereof our people fynde themselves abandoned to utter ruine and miserie.

" You shall therefor repair to the king, and, by the means of our ambassador, require speedy access, at which time you may plainly declare unto him the generalities above mentioned ; and you shall also furnish yourself with an abstract of all the mayne wronges newly done us, and deliver to the king how much it troubleth us to be requyted with nothing but continual frutes of spoyles and injuries, where we have ever sown continuall care and kyndness ; and if it may be deemed that we do less value the estate of those poor creatures who are more remote from us, than of others who daily are in compasse of our eye, surely they shall be deceived ; for in our care for their preservation, (over whom God hath constituted us equally the only head and ruler) wee never do admit any inequality or difference of care, either for point of justice to be administered by ourselves, or satisfaction to be procured from them that any way oppress them.

" But we do see that tyme spends on to their loss, that our people are vexed, our commissioners are tyred, and our selve delayed ; an therefor we require you, seeing all promises are so little observed, and all references to conventions so partially conducted, to let the king know that we cannot deny the just and pitifull appeals which our dear people make for protection and redress, but will enable them to make these unruly rabble of outlawes and ra   know and feel that they shall taste of a sourer neighbourhood than

officers to England, (page cxiv) where, however, they were not long detained.

It was not, therefore, until the union of the crowns, that any material alteration took place in the manner or customs of the Borders. Upon that great event, the forces of both countries acting with more uniform good understanding, as now the servants of the same master, suppressed every disorder of consequence. The most intractable Borderers were formed into a body of troops, which Buccleuch conducted to the Belgick wars. The Border counties were disarmed, excepting such weapons as were retained by gentlemen of rank and repute.* And the moss-troopers, who continued to exercise

---

they have done of late, seeing they do nothing but insult upon our toleration of many injuries, whilst we are apt, (out of respect to the king only) to quietness."

* Amongst other articles agreed upon betwixt the English and Scottish commissioners for the final pacification of the Borders, 9th April, 1605, after recommending that all deadly feuds should be put to agreement, or those who refused to acquiesce should be detained prisoners, that heavy mulcts and penalties should be inflicted on such Scottishmen and English as broke the peace by any act of violence, and that robbers from either country should be punished with death, there is a clause of the following tenor : " Also, it is agreed that proclamation shall be made, that all inhabiting within Tindale and Riddesdale in Northumberland, Bewcastledale, Wilgavey, the north part of Gilsland, Esk and Leven in Cumberland, East and West Tevidale, Liddesdale, Eskdale, Ewsdale and Annerdale in Scotland, (saving noblemen and gentlemen unsuspected of felony or theft, and not being of broken clans,) and their household servants dwelling within those several places before recited, shall put away all armour and weapons, as well offensive as defensive, as jacks, spears, lances, swords, daggers, steelcaps, hagbuts, pistols, plate sleeves, and such like: and shall not keep any horse, gelding, or mare, above the price of 50s. sterling, or 30l. Scots, upon like pain of imprisonment.

" Item, That proclamation be made, that none of what calling soever, within the countries lately called the Borders, of either of the kingdoms, shall wear, carry, or bear any pistols, hagbuts, or guns of any sort, but in his majesty's service, upon pain of imprisonment, according to the laws of either kingdom."

their former profession, experienced in great numbers the unsparing and severe justice of the Earl of Dunbar.

But though the evil was remedied for the present, the root remained ready to sprout upon the least encouragement. In the civil wars of Charles I., the Borderers resumed their licentious habits, particularly after the war had been transferred to Scotland, and the exploits of the moss-troopers flourish in the diaries and military reports of the time.* In the reign of Charles II. we learn their existence still endured, by the statutes directed against them.† And it is said that

---

* In a letter from Cromwell's head-quarters, Edinburgh, October 16, 1650, the exploits of the Borderers in their old profession are alluded to. " My last told you of a letter to be sent to Colonels Kerr and Straughan from hence. Satturday the 26, the commissary-general dispatcht away a trumpet with that letter, as also gave another to the Sheriff of Cumberland, to be speeded away to M. John Scot, builiff, and B. brother to the Lord of Buccliew, for his demanding restitution upon his tenants, the moss-troopers, for the horses by them stolne the night we quartered in their country, since which, promises hath been made of restitution, and we doubt not to receive it very suddenly, or else to take satisfaction another way ourselves." In the accounts of Monk's campaigns, given in the News Letter of the time, there is frequent mention of the moss-troopers.

† The 13th and 14th Charles II., ch. 3,—18th Charles II., ch. 3 and 29, and 30th Charles II. ch. 1., all proceed upon similar preambles, stating, in substance,—" Whereas a great number of lewd, disorderly, and lawless persons, being thieves and robbers, who are commonly called *moss-troopers*, have successively, for many and sundry years last past, been bred, resided in, and frequented the Borders of the two respective counties of Northumberland and Cumberland, and the most adjacent parts of Scotland; and they, taking the opportunity of the large waste ground, heaths, and mosses, and the many intricate and dangerous ways and by-paths in those parts, do usually, after the most notorious crimes committed by them, escape over from the one kingdom to the other respectively, and so avoid the hand of justice, in regard the offences done and perpetrated in the one kingdom cannot be punished in the other.

" And whereas, since the time of the late unhappy distractions, such offences and offenders as aforesaid have exceedingly more increased and abounded; and the several inhabitants of the said respective counties have been, for divers years last past, necessitated, at their own free and voluntary charge, to maintain several parties of horse for the

non-conforming presbyterian preachers were the first who brought this rude generation to any sense of the benefits of religion.✱ How-

---

necessary defence of their persons, families, and goods, and for bringing the offenders to justice." Upon this preamble follow orders for assessing the inhabitants of these disturbed counties in the sums necessary to pay sufficient bands of men for protection of the inhabitants. These acts are still in force.

✱ This appears from a curious passage in the Life of Richard Cameron, who gave name to the sect of Cameronians. After he was licensed, they sent him at first to preach in Annandale. He said, How could he go there? He knew not what sort of people they were. But Mr. Welch said, Go your way, Ritchie, and set the fire of hell to their tails. He went, and the first day he preached upon that text, *How shall I put thee among the children*, &c. In the application he said, Put you among the children! the offspring of robbers and thieves. Many have heard of Annandale thieves.—Some of them got a merciful cast that day, and told it afterwards, that it was the first field-meeting that ever they attended; and that they went out of curiosity to see how a minister could preach in a tent, and people sit on the ground."—HARRIES' *Scottish Worthies*, p. 361.

Cleland also, the poet of the sect of Cameronians, takes credit for the same conversion, and puts the following verses into the mouth of a prelatist haranguing the Highlanders, and warning them against the inconvenient strictness of the presbyterian preachers :—

> If their doctrine there get rooting,
> Then farewell theift, the best of booting,
> And this ye see is very clear,
> Duyly experience makes it appear;
> For instance, lately on the Borders,
> Where there was nought but theft and murders,
> Rapine, cheating, and resetting,
> Slight-of-hand—fortunes getting;
> Their designation, as ye ken,
> Was all along, the *Tacking Men*.
> Now rebels more prevails with words,
> Then drawgoons does with guns and swords,
> So that their bare preaching now,
> Makes the rush-bush keep the cow
> Better than Scots or English kings
> Could do by kilting them with strings;

ever this may be, there seems little doubt that, until the union of the crowns, the manners of these districts retained a tincture of their former rudeness, and would have relapsed, had occasion offered, into their former ferocity. Since that fortunate æra, all that concerns the military habits, customs, and manners of what were once the frontier counties, fall under the province into which these details may serve to introduce the reader—the study, namely, of BORDER ANTIQUITIES.

Yea, those that were the greatest rogues,
Follows them over hills and bogues,
Crying for mercy and for preaching,
For they'll now hear no others teaching.

CLELAND'S *Poems*, 1697, p. 30.

REMAINS OF

MORPETH CASTLE, NORTHUMBERLAND.

London, Published Nov.¹ 1814, for the Proprietors by Longman & C.º Paternoster Row.

BORDER ANTIQUITIES

OF

𝕰𝖓𝖌𝖑𝖆𝖓𝖉 𝖆𝖓𝖉 𝕾𝖈𝖔𝖙𝖑𝖆𝖓𝖉

DELINEATED.

𝕸𝖔𝖗𝖕𝖊𝖙𝖍 𝕮𝖆𝖘𝖙𝖑𝖊.

This ancient baronial edifice is now in ruins, its halls are desolate, and its ramparts are mouldering into dust; its accompaniments of war have crumbled away beneath the withering hand of time, and nothing scarcely remains but a few melancholy vestiges, which faintly denote the martial structure which once frowned defiance upon the enemies of its lord, and once rung with the merriment of his friends. He whose mind is imbued with those feelings which the recollection of past times is so apt to engender: he who remembers, with kindred emotion, the ages that are gone by, and all the circumstances by which they are endeared to an imagination but slightly tinctured with enthusiasm, cannot investigate, without a sigh, the fallen splendour of knightly and chivalrous periods; cannot retrace, without dejection, even though only in fancy, the era when all that romantic illusion which then belonged to the profession of arms, shed a sort of elevated character upon it, and which, in modern times, it so essentially wants. Connected with these feelings, is the melancholy sentiment with which we are naturally disposed to view the dilapidated edifices which were the chosen scenes of all those feats; and while the reader learns their fate, he indulges in a generous regret, that " the days of chivalry are gone."

Vol. I.

B

The castle, whose present and former condition we are now about to record, was distinguished, in the feudal ages of our history, as the abode of warriors, rude and unpolished, but dignified by the highest feelings of military and courtly honour. Little remains of it now, however, except an old gateway, tower, and part of the outward wall, which enclosed the area and interior buildings. Its local advantages are derived entirely from nature, being placed on a lofty eminence, about a quarter of a mile south of the town; its southern side is very steep, and washed by the river Wansbeck: the northern side is secured by a deep valley. The tower formerly had angular turrets at the north and south-east corners, with a communication by an open gallery, which was supported by projecting corbels. There is no portcullis. It is built of squared stone; and there are stairs in it ascending to the top, from whence there is a most delightful prospect, overlooking the town of Morpeth, and the banks of Wansbeck, where large tracts of woodlands are beautifully disposed. The part of the castle which remains seems to have been the gate-house. Near the tower, north-west of the gate, and about a hundred yards distant, there is a round *mound of earth*, on a natural mount, whose height is greatly increased by art. It appears to have been raised, not as an outwork or defence to the castle, but by assailants; for it must have been easy to throw from thence, by engines, stones and missile weapons into the interior parts of the fortress, which would annoy the garrison. Perhaps, indeed, according to the modes practised in early times, this was cast up for an opposing fort and *malvoisin* on some blockade.

From the extent of the bounding walls, which are still left standing, and from the traces of former buildings, this castle seems to have been, when entire, a considerable edifice, both for strength and for extent. It appears, likewise, that it was a place of strength as late as the reign of King Charles I. when it was occupied by the Scots army, who, according to a pamphlet printed in 1644, were driven from thence by the Marquis of Montrose, as also from the fortresses of South Shields, Durham, Lumley castle, Blythe-rock, and other places near Sunderland.

There is no record extant which mentions who was the founder of this castle. Early in the time of the Normans, the baronial seat of the Merleys was here, and perhaps they possessed a strong hold upon the very eminence where the present ruins stand. The tower was built by William Lord Greystock, who lived in the reign of Edward III. as appears by the escheats of that reign. He died at Branspeth, in the bishopric of Durham, in the year 1358, the 32d Edward III. He likewise built the castle of Greystock. Surnames were derived from places, and that of *Merley*, was probably derived from their fortress here. By the rolls of Henry V. the barony is called the *barony of Marlay*, whence it may be inferred, that *Merley* and *Morpeth* were places which originally were distinct from each other, the one denoting the hill and the other the valley. Afterwards, the distinctions merged in the general appellation of Morpeth.

Whatever claims, however, the family of the Merleys may have to be considered as the founders of this edifice, it is certain that its possession, as well as the estate, came into the family of Greystock, in whose issue it remained, till, the male line failing, it was carried into the family of the Dacres, about the beginning of the reign of Henry VIII. by Elizabeth Baroness of Greystock, who married Thomas Lord Dacre of Gisland. It afterwards passed, about the time of Elizabeth, into the family of Howard, by the marriage of Anne, one of the last co-heirs of George, the last Lord Dacre, with William Howard, third son of Thomas Duke of Norfolk. It still remains in his descendants, being now the property of the Right Hon. Frederick Earl of Carlisle, a nobleman distinguished no less for his private worth than for his public talents.

In Leland's time, Morpeth castle was entire, as may be inferred from his description of it, which is as follows:

" Morpet, a market town, is xii. long myles from Newcastle. Wansbecke, a praty ryver, rynnithe throwghe the syde of the towne. On the hethar syde of the ryver, is the principall church of the towne: on the same syde is the fayre castle stondinge upon a hill, longinge, with the towne, to the Lord Dacres of Gelstand." He adds, " Morpith castle stondythe by Morpeth towne; it is set on a highe hill, and about the hille is muche woode. The towne and castle belongeth to the Lord Dacors. It is well mayntayned."

Castle at Newcastle.

It is agreed by all writers who have described this venerable pile, that its antiquity is as remote as the period of the Norman conquest; that period which is adorned in our imaginations with all the splendour that chivalry and gallant enterprise bestow upon past events. Its founder was Robert Carthouse, son of William the Conqueror, and the era of its foundation 1080, on his return from his Scotch expedition; whence the town took the name of Newcastle, for, previously to that event, it was called Monkchester. Robert de Carthouse perceived the local advantages which combined to render such a structure beneficial; for, placed on the frontiers of the two countries, commanding the course of so fine a river, and admirably adapted for the assembling of levies in the event of any border irruption, it would be at once the protection and ornament of the place.

The tower, as built by Robert, was of great strength; square, and surrounded by two walls. The height of the tower is eighty-two feet, the square on the outside sixty-two feet by fifty-four, the walls thirteen feet thick, and with galleries gained out of them. Within the tower there was a chapel, but such is the silent potency of time, and such the vain efforts of man even in his most stupendous undertakings, that all that was once the outward defence to this place of strength is now defaced, and the site crowded with modern buildings, occupied by persons devoted to pursuits far different from those which busied the minds of the warlike inhabitants of the middle ages. The tower, however, still remains entire, and the corners of it project from the plane of the square, a mode of architecture much practised in Norman buildings. Its situation, on a lofty eminence, was admirably adapted to the purposes of its erection, that of overawing and commanding, not only the whole town, but remotely, in the facilities for warfare which it afforded, the surrounding country. Its principal entrance was to the south, but the exact number of gates contained in the outward walls cannot now be precisely determined, except perhaps from Bourne's account, which will be presently mentioned. The area inclosed by

THE CASTLE, AT NEWCASTLE; NORTHUMBERLAND

Engraved by J.R. Greig from a Painting by L.T. 1808 with Antiquities in England and Scotland.

London Published March 1st 1814, for the Proprietors by Longman & Co. Paternoster Row.

the wall contained three acres and one rood. The castle belongs to the county of Northumberland, and forms no part of the liberties of Newcastle or of its sheriffdom.

On the 21st Sept. 1st Henry VII. the office of constable of this castle was granted to William Case, Esq. for life, with the usual salary and fees; and in the 9th of the same reign, it being vacant by the death of Sir Robert Moulton, it was granted to Roger Fenwick, Esq. for life, with twenty pounds per annum. Since that period no constable has been appointed, but it has remained in the custody of the sheriffs of Northumberland. It now serves for the county prison, and in the great hall the judges of assize hold the gaol delivery.

The castle had not been long erected before it was destined to prove its value as a fortification and as a place of defence. Bourne says, that Robert de Mowbray, Earl of Northumberland, was besieged in it by William Rufus, during the rebellion that was stirred up against that monarch, by his haughty, discontented, and turbulent nobles. The fortress suffered much damage, and was finally taken. There is, however, some doubt entertained by antiquaries and historians, as to the fidelity of this account by Bourne, as it is not supported by adequate authorities. In the first year of King Stephen, (1135), the Scots gained possession of the castle and tower by treachery, and held it theirs till 1156, when Malcolm the IV. ceded all the northern counties to King Henry II.

During this period, which we have thus gone through, the castle sustained much injury by external attack, and was, likewise, silently dilapidating through neglect: when King John not only restored it to its former state, but added a ditch to the fortifications. In doing this, however, he was compelled to destroy many houses, and, unwilling to commit any arbitrary act of oppression in a petty cause, though willing to be a tyrant in a greater one, he ordered a compensation to be made to the owners of those houses—viz. 110s. 6d. rents in escheats to be paid yearly; and this he set forth and confirmed in his charter to the town of Newcastle.

Of such importance was this castle considered, in a rude and warlike age, when civilization was so tardy that the strong arm of government itself was too feeble to repress injuries and revolts, and in a country where predatory irruptions were constantly made by the neighbouring Scots, that most of the surrounding baronies were willing to pay considerable sums towards its sup-.

port, under the articles castleward and cornage. The various sums are minutely specified in Bourne; and the names of the baronies which paid them were the following :—

The barony of Herons,	The barony of Dilston,
——————Walton,	——————Bolbeck,
——————Bolam,	——————Gaugie,
——————Marley,	——————Bothal,
——————Delaval,	——————Rosse,
——————Bywell,	——————Copun.

Besides the larger sums paid by these baronies, several smaller ones were contributed by divers houses, yards, and gardens.

The most exact and satisfactory account which we possess of this building is to be found in Bourne's History of Newcastle, and which, as it is both curious and interesting, we shall here copy.

" In the ninth year of King Edward III." says he, " an inquisition was taken at this town, whereby it was found, that at the time of the battle of Bannockburn, which was in the year 1313, when John de Venont, knight, was high-sheriff of Northumberland, this castle, and all its edifices about it, were in good repair; that after that time Nicholas Scot, Adam de Swinburne, William Riddel, Johannes de Fenwick, Cuthbert de Broughdon, Johannes de Fenwick, Johannes de Woodhorn, Johannes de Lilleburn, Willielmus de Tynedale, Roger Mauduit, and Robertus Darreius, were high-sheriffs of Northumberland, during which time the great tower and also the lesser ones of the said castle, the great hall, with the king's chamber adjoining to it, together with divers other chambers below, in the queen's mantle, and the buttery, cellar, and pantry; the king's chapel within the castle, a certain house beyond the gate, which is called the chequer house, with the bridges within and without the gate, with three gates and one postern, were 300*l*. worse than before. They also say that there are in the custody of Roger Mauduit, late high-sheriff, 420 fother of lead; they say also that it was thought highly necessary that the Baron Heron of Huddeston, the Baron of Walton, Lord Robert Clifford, of the New Place, chief lord of the barony of Gaugie, the lords of the barony of————— and Devilston, that the Lord of Werk upon Tweed, the lord of the barony of Bolbeck, alias Bywell, the Baron of Rothal, and lastly the Baron of Delaval, should build, each of them, a house within the liberties of the castle, for the defence of it.

There were two great strong walls which surrounded the castle; the interior wall was of no great distance from the castle itself, as may be still seen in several places. The exterior wall surrounds the verge of the castle borders; from this outer wall were four gates, the great gate and three posterns. The north side of the castle is the main gate, called now the Black gate: it had two portcullises, one without the gate, as may still be seen, and another within, at a little distance from it, the ruins of which were to be seen a few years ago. There still remains a piece of the old wall, which shews its situation to have been where that house is which was lately purchased by Mr. Jasper Harrison. The shop belonging to this house was dug (as I am informed) out of the wall just now mentioned. On the east side of the castle there was a postern, which led down to the street called the Side, which is still to be seen: it was once called (but many years after it was in decay) the Waist of Laurentius Acton. On the south side of the castle is another gate which leads down the castle stairs to the street called the Close: this was the south postern. There is a building upon it which was the county gaoler's house. On the west side was the postern facing Bailiff's gate, now the dwelling-house of James Lidster.

" There is an house in the yard which they say was the chapel of the garrison, which is called the chapel house to this day: it stands north-east from the chapel; its common name now is the Three Bulls' Heads."

By an inquisition made in the reign of James I. it appears this castle was at that period greatly out of repair; and, in the 18th of the same reign, another inquisition being taken, complaint was then made that a large dunghill which was heaped up against the wall on the west side of the castle had done damage to the amount of 120*l.* It was also complained by the said inquisition, that the great square tower was full of chinks and crannies, and that one third of it was almost taken away; that all the lead and coverings which it had of old were embezzled and carried off, so that " the prisoners of the county of Northumberland were most miserably lodged, by reason of the showers of rain falling upon them." The charge of repairing all this was computed at 809*l.* 15*s.* The dunghill above-mentioned was removed in 1644, by Sir John Morley, and used to make a rampart on the town-walls against the Scots, and the round tower under the moot-hall, now called the half-moon, was repaired by him for the same purpose.

" It has been," continues Bourne, " a building of great strength and no little beauty; the vast thickness of the walls speaks the one, and the ruins of some curious workmanship, the other. The grand entrance into the castle was at this gate, facing the south, which leads up a pair of stairs (which still shew the magnificence of the builder) to a very stately door of curious masonry. The room which this leads into has its floor broken down close to the castle wall, as indeed all other floors are, to the top of the castle: so that, excepting the floor above the county gaol, there is not one left, though there have been five divisions or stories of the castle beside this. This floored room, which I was told was lately flagged by the order of William Ellison, Esq. alderman, when he was last mayor, in the year 1723, seems to me, without any doubt, to have been the common hall of the castle, because, on the north side of the same room there is an entrance, by a descent of some steps, into a room where is the largest fire-place I saw in the castle, which plainly speaks it to have been the kitchen. At the end of this there are several stairs, which lead into a place under the kitchen, which I think goes down as low as the bottom of the castle; this I take to have been a cellar, as I do also that little dark place on the right hand coming up again, to have been a sort of pantry. The door I mentioned just now on the east of the castle, which leads to the first broken-down floor, is, because of its grandeur and beauty, an argument that this room has been the most stately one in the whole castle; another reason for its being so is, because of the windows which gave light into it. Those of them that face the east are the most beautiful of the whole castle besides. On the south of this room there is an entrance into a sort of parlour, or withdrawing-room, which has a fire-place in it; which has been a piece of curious workmanship, as is visible to this day; and this place has no communication with any part of the castle but this room. On the north side of this room is a door leading into an apartment where stands a well of considerable depth; it was eighteen yards before we touched the surface of the water, which seems to have been placed there on purpose for the more immediate service of this room. There are some little basins on the top of the well, with pipes leading from them, which conveyed water to different apartments of the castle: this is plain, from what may be observed in the county gaol, at the bottom of the castle; the round stone pillar in it having an hollow, in the middle, of a foot wide, with a lead spout in the side of it.

Engraved by J.ᵐᶜ Greig, from a Painting by L.Clennell, for the Border Antiquities of England and Scotland.

AN ORNAMENTED DOORWAY IN THE
CASTLE, at NEWCASTLE; NORTHUMBERLAND.

London Publish'd May 1.ˢᵗ 1812, for the Proprietors by Longman & Cᵒ Paternoster Row.

Engraved by J. Greig from a Drawing by L. Clennell for the Border Antiquities of England & Scotland.

Part of the INTERIOR of the
CASTLE AT NEWCASTLE,
Northumberland.

London Published Sep.t 1814, for the Proprietors, by Longman & C.º Paternoster Row.

"In the inquisition made in the 9th of Edward III. above-mentioned, among other things that were complained of for being neglected, was *capella domini regis infra castrum.* This chapel, I have been told, stood on that part of the castle-yard where the moot-hall is, but, upon searching, I found it in the castle itself, according to the account of it just now mentioned. The door of it is at the bottom of the south wall of the castle, joining to the stairs which lead into the state chamber. It has been a work of great beauty and ornament, and is still, in the midst of dust and darkness, by far the most beautiful place in the whole building, the inside of it being curiously adorned with arches and pillars. It is easy to observe the different parts of it; the entrance, the body, and the chancel: on the left side of the entrance you go into a dark little room, which undoubtedly was the vestry; the full length of it is fifteen yards, the breadth of it six yards and a half. It had three or four windows towards the east, which are now all filled up, nor is there any light but what comes in at a little cranny in the wall. *Nicholas de Byker, tenet terras suas ut faciat destructiones ad ward novi castelli super Tynam, facient' et pro deb' domini regis inter Tynam et Cocket, &c.* And then my authority goes on to say, that the manor of Byker was Sir Ralph Lawson's, knight, deceased; after of Henry Lawson, Esq. his son; and now of his eldest son; who, without all question, is bailiff by inheritance, of the said castle, and is to levy the castle-ward, cornage, &c. and other rents, issues, fines, and amercements belonging to the said castle; and, as he goes on, the constable of the castle when that office is settled, may appoint the learned steward to keep courts; and then the offices of the said castle will be complete. Besides the rent above-mentioned, a great number of houses, yards, and gardens, paid to it. The act of resumption, 1st Henry VIII. on the rolls of parliament, has an exception in favour of William Case, then constable of the castle of Newcastle upon Tyne.

"In the 17th James I. 1619, a grant was made of the site and demesnes of the castle, to Alexander Stevenson, Esq. who was succeeded by one Patrick Black, who died and left it in the possession of his wife. After that, one James Langton, Gent. claimed Patrick Black's right, but by virtue of what is not known. The liberties and privileges of the castle extend northwards to the river Tweed, and southward to the river of Tees.

"It is reported that underneath that house which was anciently the county jail, was a vault which leads to the castle; there is, indeed, a large door still to be seen, which perhaps was the entrance into it; and Mr. George Grey, the present possessor of the house, told me it was certainly so, because he had put down, through his own floor, a bailiff's rod, to the very end, and could find no bottom.

"A MS. I have had often occasion to mention, gives us the following account of the castle yard:—'The way through the yard begins at the castle gate, and when I was young, there was no house in it but the house of one Thomas Southern, and the house of one Green. These houses were near the gate before you come into the castle yard, and there was in the garth, a house wherein the gaoler of the castle dwelt, and a house wherein William Robinson dwelt, who was deputy herald unto Norroy K. at arms: this man wrote in a book the arms of all the mayors of this town, from Laurentius Acton until his time, and when I was chamberlain of the town, which was about the time of Sir Nicholas Cole being mayor, in 1640, it was then in the town's chamber; when Trollop built the town-court, he borrowed it and never restored it.'"

At the time mentioned there were no other houses than those; but since that period Mr. Bulmer took a garth behind his house, in the side, and built a stable, and had a garden in it. George Hayroy also took from thence to the moot-hall, and built houses upon it. The building of the castle gate was begun by one Alexander Stephenson, a Scotsman, who came into England with King James, but it was finished by one John Pickle, exactly in that style of architecture in which it now appears: he also kept a tavern in it. After that, one Jordan, a Scotsman also, and *sword kipper*, built the house on the south side of this gate, and occupied it; and Thomas Reed, a Scots pedlar, took a shop in the north side of the gate.

At present there are a great many shops and houses belonging to it, in and about it.

In the year 1737, 10th George II., the site and demesnes of the castle were granted to George Riddle, Esq. for fifty years, from the 2d July, 1736: rent, one hundred chaldron of coals for Greenwich hospital.

Many of the old houses which encumbered the remains of this castle have recently been taken down, and considerable improvements are now going on at Newcastle. The castle is to be preserved from further dilapidations with the utmost care.

ENTRANCE TO THE

CASTLE GARTH NEWCASTLE,

Northumberland.

WARKWORTH CASTLE,

Northumberland.

Engraved by J. Greig from a Drawing by E. Dayes, for the Border Antiquities of England & Scotland.

London, Published Aug.t 1st 1817 for the Proprietors, by Longman & Co. Paternoster Row

𝖂arkworth 𝖈astle.

THIS stately and venerable structure stands on a lofty eminence adjoining to the south end of the town of Warkworth, from which there is a pleasing, though steep approach to the castle : this access gives the fortress an august appearance. Its west side commands a view of the river Coquet. " Nothing," says Grose, " can be more magnificent and picturesque, from what part soever it is viewed ; and though when entire it was far from being destitute of strength, yet its appearance does not excite the idea of one of those rugged fortresses destined solely for war, whose gloomy towers suggest to the imagination only dungeons, chains, and executions ; but rather that of such an ancient hospitable mansion as is alluded to by Milton :

> " Where throngs of knights, and barons bold,
> In weeds of peace high triumphs hold.

" Or, as is described in our old romances, where, in the days of chivalry, the wandering knight or distressed princess found honourable reception and entertainment, the holy palmer, repose for his wearied limbs, and the poor and helpless, their daily bread."

The castle stands on the crown of a rock, and is of an oblong figure : the great tower to the north, placed on the brink of the cliff, above the town, is of fine architecture, in chisel-work, and of a singular figure, being octangular. From the centre of four opposite sides, a turret projects of a semi-hexagonal form, and from the middle of the building a very lofty exploratory turret arises. This part of the castle owes its origin to the Percys, as is evident from the lion of Brabant, which is above the gate, and also from the arms which are dispersed over the whole building. The western side is formed of various irregular towers and walling of different ages, extending along the brink of the cliff, whose foot is washed by the river Coquet. On the south, the ground gradually ascends to the elevation of the rocks, on which the western buildings are founded. The front of this side of the castle opens to a spacious plain or platform, and is defended by a lofty wall, with an outward moat. On this side are the ancient gateway, and chief entrance to the castle: the gate is defended by a circular tower and drawbridge. The eastern side is placed on the brink of a steep declivity, defended by an outward moat and a lofty wall, guarded by a square bastion near the centre, as well as by an angular tower at the south point. The walls enclose a spacious area, almost square, and within which the ancient parts of the fortress are in a state of great dilapidation.

According to an ancient survey, the castle and moat contained five acres, seventeen perches and a half of ground. The keep, or dungeon, forms the north front; its figure is a square, with the angles canted off. Near the middle of each fall of this square there is a turret, which projects at right angles, with its end terminating in a semi-hexagon. These projections are of the same height as the rest of the keep. The keep itself is very large and lofty, and contains a variety of magnificent apartments: above it, there rises a high watch-tower, commanding an almost unbounded prospect. On the north side next the street, there are several figures of angels, bearing armorial shields; and at the top of the turret there is carved, in the middle, a large lion rampant in bas relief.

When Leland wrote his *Itinerary*, this castle was in thorough repair: his words are, " Warkworth castle stondeth on the side of Coquet water: it is well maynteyned and is large." At that period also the Percy family was under attainder, and Warkworth castle was in the hands of the crown; where, probably, it was neglected, and fell into that decay which is described in a survey that was taken about the year 1567, after the family had been but a few years restored. This survey, as it is a curious document, and as it contains particulars interesting to the antiquary, and even to the general reader, we shall present to our readers. It is extracted from Grose's Antiquities, to whom it was communicated, by permission of their graces the Duke and Duchess of Northumberland, it being preserved among the archives of that illustrious house. We shall first, however, endeavour to convey some idea of the charming and varied scenery which environs this venerable mansion, and which adds all the attractive beauties of nature to the grander efforts of art.

The view from the castle is so extensive and so various, that we are con-

Engraved by T... ...ing from a Painting by L. Peacock for the Beauties Antiquities of England & Scotland.

ENTRANCE TO

WARKWORTH CASTLE, NORTHUMBERLAND.

London Publish'd May 1 1824 for the Proprietors, by Longman & Co Paternoster Row.

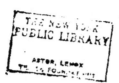

KEEP OF
WARKWORTH CASTLE,
Northumberland.

Engraved by T. Barry from a Drawing by J. Greenwood, for the Durable Antiquities of England & Scotland.

London, Published Sep.r 1st. by the Proprietors, by Longman & C.o Paternoster Row.

scious it will not be in the power of words to impress any thing like an adequate notion of it upon the mind of the reader: nor, had we even the graphic
powers of a Denham, a Pope, or a Thomson, should we hope to make it,

"Live in description and look green in song."

To the north and north-east the sea stretches out in grand perspective,
while its level uniformity is relieved by the Farn Islands, which lie scattered
over its surface. In a nearer view is the port of Alemouth, and a little
beyond that are seen the mouth of the river Coquet and Coquet island, where
the imagination has a pleasing field for solemn thought, in contemplating
the ruins of its ancient monastery. To the north extends a rich and cultivated country as far as Alnwick; while to the west the eye is delighted with
the view of the Coquet river, the winding channel of which is adorned and
variegated by small spots of woodland. On the south there is an extensive
plain, gently sloping towards the sea, covered with villages, smiling beneath
the fruitful industry of man, and interspersed with the more solemn and august
beauty of woods and forests. The whole shore is indented with many small
ports and creeks: the uplands are thickly covered with innumerous hamlets,
churches, and other buildings, producing a charming scene of various landscape; while in the furthest distance the different tints arising from remoter
objects, produce, altogether, a prospect which neither language nor the
pencil can adequately pourtray. The spectator who beholds it, may exclaim
in the language of our descriptive bard,

> Heavens! what a goodly prospect spreads around,
> Of hills, and dales, and woods, and lawns, and spires,
> And glittering towers and gilded streams, till all
> The stretching landscape into smoke decays!
> Happy Britannia! where the Queen of Arts
> Inspiring vigour, Liberty abroad
> Walks unconfin'd, e'en to thy farthest cots,
> And scatters plenty with unsparing hand.

The castle, but more especially the buildings in the outer court, falling
into great decay, a warrant was granted to Mr. Whitehead,* one of the
Earl of Northumberland's stewards, dated June 24, 1608, " to take down

---

* Taken from an entry made in a book containing copies of commissions, &c. on the Earl of
Northumberland's affairs.

the lead that lieth upon the ruinous towers and places of Warkworth, to way it and lay it uppe, and to certify his lordship of the quantity thereof, that the places where lead is taken off be covered again, for the preservation of the timber." In 1610, accordingly, the old timber of the buildings in the outer court was sold, for twenty-eight pounds.

In 1672 the dungeon, or keep of the castle, was unroofed, at the instance of Joseph Clarke,* one of the auditors to the family, who obtained a gift of the materials from the then Countess of Northumberland. The following is a copy of a letter from him to one of his tenants.

"William Milbourne:—Being to take down the materials of Warkworth castle, which are given me by the Countess of Northumberland, to build a house at Chenton, I doe desire you to speak to all her ladishipp's tenantes in Warkeworth, Birlinge, Buston, Acklington, Shilbottle, Lesbury, Longhanton, and Bilton, that they will assist me with their draughts as soone as conveniently they can, to remove the lead and tymber which shall be taken downe, and such other materials as shall be fitt to be removed, and bringe it to Chenton, which will be an obligation to there and your friend,

"Newcastle, 27 April, 1672.　　　　　　　　　"Jo. Clarke.

"To my loving friende William Milbourne,
　　　at his house at Birlinge."

We shall now present our readers with that survey of this castle to which we have already alluded, and for which we are indebted to Grose's *Antiquities*.

Extract from a Survey by Geo. Clarkson, 1565.

"The castell of Warkworth ys situate on the ryver Cockett: on the south syde of the same ryver ys one little mount, parteley maid by nature of the ground, with the course of the sayd ryver on the west syde, and on the east and north syde with moytes casten and made by mens worke; and one the sowth parte ys the way and passadge to and from the sayd castell by two severall ways; one of the which two passadges were good to be mad use; that ys the way that goyth towards the sowth by the loyninge were most expedyent; thendes of the sayd loyninge strongly ditched, casten, or made

---

* One of the auditors to the then Earl of Northumberland.

with stone wall, and the hye streate to be made to goo thorow the demaynes, and the same casten in a loyning there with a strong quick woode hedge, casten of eyther syde; the stones of th' old cawsey taken awaye, and a cawsey newly made within that ground of the sayde demaynes, viz. from the north end of a meadow-close called Tybbettes close eastward, to one hye waye that goyth to the gate of the demaynes, and along the same waye to the sayd gate; which might be done with small charge; and that done, the parke wold not only be on that syde well inclosed, the dear have feedinge nighe the gate of the sayd castell, but also yt shold be a great strength to the sayd parke, castell, and groundes joyninge upon the same, a better passadge than that now ys in all respects, and hurt no person, so that the same were well and orderlye done or made.

"The buyldinge of the sayd castell on the sowth parte, is thre towres: viz. the gate-house towres, in the middle thereof; which is th' entrye at a draw-bridge over drye moyte; and in the same towre ys a prison, and porter lodge; and over the same a fare lodginge, called the constables lodgings, and in the cour layne between the gate-house and west towre in the corner beynge round of diverse squares, called Cradyfurgus, is a fare and comely buyldinge, a chapell, and diverse howses of office one the ground; and above the great chambre, and the lordes lodginge: all which be now in great decay, as well in the coverleur beynge lead, as also in tymbere and glass; and without some help of reparaciones it will come to utter ruin.

"Turning north from the south-west corner in that courtayn streatchinge to another little towre, called the posterne towre, ys th' old hall, which was verie fare, and now by reason yt was in decay, ys vnroofed, and the tymbre taken downe lyinge in the said castell. In the same square a but-trye, pantrye, and kitchinge, which are now in utter decay. And at th' entrye into the hall, for the porche thereof, is raysed a little square towre, wherein is two chambers, and on the fore syd in stone portrayed a lyon very workemanly wrought, and therefore called the lyon towre; the same is covered with lead, and in good reparacions. Th' other towre, called the posterne towre, is two lodginges, under which goith out a posterne; and the same is covered with lead, and in good reparacions. In th' est syde of the great hall was an ile sett owt with pyllers, which yet standeth, and covered with lead. From the gate-howse towre to the towre in th' est corner, called ——————,

ys no buyldinge, but onely a curtayne wall, fare and of a new buyldinge;
and in that towre is a stable one the ground, and thre lodginge above: the
same is covered with lead, and in good reparacions. Turnyng from that
towre towards the doungeon north, is another little turret in the wall, ys sett
upon that courteyn wall, stables and gardeners over the same covered with
slate, and in good reparacions. Over the courte from the sayd towre,
called the Posterne Towre, to the said turrett, ys the foundacion of a house
which was ment to have been a colledge, and good parte of the walls were
builded; which yf yt had bene finished and made a parfit square, the same
had been a division betweene the said courte to the lodgings before recyted,
and the dungeon. The buildinge that was made of the sayd colledge is now
taken awaye, saving that certeyn walls under the ground thereof yet remayne:
and at th' est part thereof is now a brewhouse and bakhouse, coverd with
slate, and in good reparacions. In the sayd courte, is a drawell which
serveth the holle house of water. The dongion is in the north parte of the
scyte of the sayd castell, sett upon a little mount highyer than the rest of the
cowrte . . . . steps of a greus before ye enter to yt: and the
same ys buyld as a foure square, and owt of every square one towre: all
which be so quarterly squared together that in the seght every parte appeareth fyve towres very finely wrought of mason worke, and in the same con-
teyned, as well a fare hall, kytchinge, and all other houses of offices verie
fare and aptly placed, as also great chambre, chapell, and lodgins for the
lord and his trayn. In the middle thereof is a peace voy'd which is called a
lanterne, which both receyveth the water from diverse spowtes of the lead,
and hath his conveyance for the same; and also gevith light to certaine lodgings in some partes. And on the part of the same at the top ys raysed of
a good hight above all the houses a turret, called the watch-house; upon the
top whereof ys a great vyew to be had, and a fare prospect, as well towards
the sea, as all parties of the land. In the north part of the sayd dungeon ys
portrayed a lyon wrought in the stone verie workmanly.

  "The castle is envyroned on thre partes with th' sayd ryver; and of the north
parte; in and angle within the sayd water, is situate a towne, called the borowgh
of Warkworth, and the parish church, and at the north end thereof a bridge over
the water, and a little towre buyld on th' end of the sayd bridge, wher a pare of
gates ys hanged.; and now the towre ys without roof, and cover; and without

amendment will in short tyme utterlye decay: yt shall be therefore very requisite that the towre be with all speed repaired, and the gates hanged upe, which shall be a great savety and comoditye for the towne."

Having thus described the ancient and modern state of this structure, we shall conclude our account of it with some notice of its various possessors.

Warkworth was formerly the barony of Roger Fitz-Richard, who held it by the service of one knight's fee. It was granted to him by King Henry II. and confirmed by Richard I. He married Eleanor, one of the daughters and co-heirs of Henry de Essex, Baron of Raleigh and Clavering, and had by her Robert, surnamed Fitz-Roger, to whom King John, in the first year of his reign, confirmed this part of the fee of inheritance, of the castle and manor of Warkworth, with the appurtenances made by his father, as beneficially and entirely as it was held by Henry I. This Robert died about the 12th of King John, leaving issue by Margaret, daughter and sole heiress of William de Caisennetto, alias Cheney, and relict of Hugh de Cressy, one son called John, and surnamed Fitz-Robert, to whom King John, in the 14th year of his reign, confirmed the castle and manor of Warkworth, to be held by the accustomed service of one knight's fee. He married Adela, heiress of Hugh de Baliol, and left at his death three sons, the eldest of whom, Roger Fitz-John, succeeded to the inheritance of his baronies and manors; he died in the 33d of Henry III. leaving issue Robert, surnamed Fitz-Roger, the second of that name, who married Margaret, daughter of the Lord de la Zouch, and dying in the 3d Edward III. left an only son, named John, who took upon him the name of Clavering.

This John de Clavering, in consideration of a grant for life of certain crown lands in the counties of Norfolk, Suffolk, and Northampton, made over to King Edward II. the reversion, in fee, of his barony and castle of Warkworth, together with other manors, provided he should die without issue male; and this reversion, King Edward III: in the 2d year of his reign, (John de Clavering being then living,) granted to Henry de Percy, and his heirs, to be held by the accustomed services; which grant was, two years afterwards, confirmed by the parliament; and John de Clavering dying that year, the King directed by his writ, dated the 24th of January, that the several baronies and manors should be delivered to him, which was accordingly done.

Warkworth castle continued in the Percy family till the 8th Richard II.

VOL. I. D

1884, when the Scots, having taken the castle of Berwick, by bribing the person to whom Henry Percy, first Earl of Northumberland, had entrusted it, the Duke of Lancaster, then a great enemy to that nobleman, accused him of treason before the Lords, and even procured his condemnation, and the consequent confiscation of his estates; but, the Earl having retaken Berwick, and made his innocence apparent, he was again restored to his honours and estates.

In the preceding reign of King Henry IV. when that king quarrelled with the Percys, who had helped him to the crown, this castle was taken from the Earl of Northumberland, and bestowed upon Sir Robert Umfreville, Knight, in whose possession it remained till the restoration of the Percy family in the succeeding reign, at the conclusion of which, during the civil wars of York and Lancaster, this great family was again attainted, being involved in the ruin which attended the house of Lancaster, to which they were firm adherents. The forfeited estates were given away to gratify some of the principal adherents to the house of York. But the storm soon blew over, and in the 12th year of Edward IV. the attainder was reversed, and the castle once more restored to the family.

They were destined, however, to undergo another reverse; for, on the death of the sixth Earl of Northumberland, they came again into the possession of the crown. Sir Thomas Percy, Knight, brother and heir to Henry Percy, the sixth Earl, having been executed and attainted for being concerned in what was called Aske's rebellion, anno 29 Henry VIII. 1538, the Earl his brother had, with a wise precaution, left all his estates to the crown, in order to keep them entire till the family should be restored.

This event soon happened: for, 1557, the Percy family was again restored to all their honours and estates, in the person of Thomas Percy, son of Sir Thomas above-mentioned, whom Queen Mary, by her letters patent, (dated 3 and 4 Philip and Mary) advanced to the dignity of Baron Percy, &c. and Earl of Northumberland. A part of these estates was Warkworth castle: but this Thomas, unfortunately engaging with the Earl of Westmoreland, in the great northern insurrection against Queen Elizabeth, in 1569, he was, after having been kept prisoner in Scotland three years, delivered up to the queen's officers in the north, and beheaded at York on the 22d August, 1572.

By virtue of the entails in the last creation, however, the titles and estates were not forfeited to the crown by the attainder of Earl Thomas; but descended to his brother Henry Percy, eighth Earl of Northumberland, and passed through his several successors, till at last the earldom became extinct, on the death of Josceline Percy, the eleventh Earl, who died without issue male in 1670 : but the baronies and estates devolved (in right of his mother the lady Elizabeth Percy, only daughter of Earl Joceline, and wife of Charles Duke of Somerset) to Algernon Seymore, Duke of Somerset, who, during the life of his father, took his seat in the House of Peers, as Baron Percy, &c. But this nobleman (having then only one daughter, Elizabeth, wife of Sir Hugh Smithson, Bart.) was, in the 23d Geo. II. 1749, created Baron Warkworth of Warkworth Castle, and Earl of Northumberland, with remainder to his son-in-law, Hugh Smithson, who, on the death of the said Duke Algernon, thus succeeded to the Earldom of Northumberland; and his lady became, in her own right, Baroness Percy, Lucy, Poinings, Fitz-Payne, Brian, and Latimer. With these titles descended the great estates of the Percy family in Northumberland, and this castle and barony of Warkworth.

𝕎arkworth Hermitage.

In perusing the history of this relic of antiquity, the mind is forcibly im-
pressed with feelings of a more tender and a more pleasing cast than are
always excited by the contemplation of architectural ruins. Such a contemplation, indeed, can rarely fail to call up associations peculiarly gratifying to
all whose natures are susceptible of those gentle and melancholy emotions
which throng about the heart when we behold before us the fallen greatness
of past times, and the frail memorials of manners, habits, and customs, upon
which the imagination loves to dwell with a sort of pious enthusiasm. The
cause of this pleasure, a pleasure which man seems almost instinctively to
feel at the sight of ruins, we will not stop to examine; the fact is decisive,
as every one can affirm by a simple reference to himself. But there are de-
grees of pleasure in this, as in every other case, arising from the habits of
early association, and in the modes of thinking peculiar to the individual.
While some would feel themselves sublimed to a height of moral energy, by
viewing the plain of Marathon, or standing in the pass of Thermopylæ, while
others would experience the same elevation of sentiment in traversing the
Holy Land, or in pausing among the ruins of Iona, and while some would
find an equal delight in beholding the remains of ancient art on the classic
shores of Greece and Rome, there are others, and they perhaps forming the
great bulk of any nation, who love to have their feelings roused by things
that " come home to their bosoms," by transactions which they can easily
comprehend, because they are such as they may all experience, and their
sympathy excited by the tender calamities of others, which are believed to be
real, because they are known to be common. Such minds, when moved by
a tale of hapless love or domestic misery, do not, perhaps, take so lofty a reach
of sentiment as those who dwell with a sort of ecstasy of thought upon the
proud records of the human race in former ages; but it may be justly doubted
whether their sensibility, if less exalted, be less exquisite or less grateful to
themselves; it may be hoped, therefore, that the account of Warkworth Her-

Engraved by J.Greig, from a Painting by L. Clennell for the Border Antiquities of England & Scotland.

WARKWORTH HERMITAGE.
Northumberland.

Pl. I.

London Published Jan. 1, 1813, for the Proprietors, by Longman & C.º Paternoster Row.

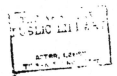

mitage, as being connected with the familiar but touching circumstances of domestic love, will not excite less interest than may have hitherto been felt in reading the history of baronial or of consecrated edifices.

Doctor Percy, in his beautiful ballad of the *Hermit of Warkworth*, a ballad which unites all the graceful simplicity of the ancient metrical romance with the polished elegance of modern poetry, has related not only the circumstances connected with the foundation of this hermitage, but has described, with the happiest effect, its scenery and local peculiarities; and it may serve to relieve the tedium of minute description, if some of those stanzas be here inserted, which refer more particularly to what will occur in the course of that description. It opens in the following picturesque manner :—

Dark was the night, and wild the storm,
  And loud the torrent's roar,
And loud the sea was heard to dash
  Against the distant shore.

Musing on man's weak hapless state
  The lonely hermit lay;

When lo! he heard a female voice
  Lament in sore dismay.

With hospitable haste he rose,
  And wak'd his sleeping fire,
And snatching up a lighted brand,
  Forth hied the reverend sire.

The following stanzas contain a very accurate, and, it will be allowed, a very poetical description of the hermitage and its adjuncts. Dr. Percy, it should be remembered, wrote from the strong impressions of actual inspection, and not from the transmitted ideas of others.

And now attended by their host,
  The hermitage they view'd,
Deep hewn within a craggy cliff,
  And overhung with good.

And near, a flight of shapely steps,
  All cut with nicest skill;
And piercing through a stony arch,
  Ran winding up the hill.

There, deck'd with many a flower and herb
  His little garden stands;
With fruitful trees in shady rows,
  All planted by his hands.

Then scoop'd within the solid rock,
  Three sacred vaults he shews;
The chief a chapel, neatly arch'd,
  On branching columns rose.

Each proper ornament was there
That should a chapel grace;
The lattice for confession fram'd,
And holy water vase.

O'er either door a sacred text
Invites to godly fear;
And in a little 'scutcheon hung
The cross, and crown, and spear.

Up to the altar's ample breadth
Two easy steps ascend;

And near, a glimmering solemn light
Two well-wrought windows lend.

Beside the altar rose a tomb,
All in the living stone,
On which a young and beauteous maid
In goodly sculpture shone.

A kneeling angel, fairly carv'd,
Lean'd hovering o'er her breast;
A weeping warrior at her feet,
And near to these her crest.

In relating the circumstances which led to the erection of this hermitage, Dr. Percy has adhered partly to truth, and has partly employed, it is believed, the pen of fiction. The tenant of the hermitage, the "lonely hermit," who received the night wanderers to his cell, is supposed to be a knight, called Sir Bertram, who had fallen in love with the daughter of a neighbouring Northumbrian chief, and who aspired to her hand in wedlock. She requited his love, and in the spirit of ancient chivalry presented him with a helm, desiring him to prove his valour by his deeds. Sir Bertram departed for the Scotish wars, and fought bravely. He was cleft down in battle, and borne almost lifeless off the field. His beloved heard of the mischance, and set out to visit him. Meanwhile he is conveyed to her castle, hears of her departure, and immediately on his recovery, not finding her returned, his brother and himself set forth by different roads to seek her through the country. The rest shall be told in Dr. Percy's own words:

'One day, as he sat under a thorn,
All sunk in deep despair,
An aged pilgrim pass'd him by
Who mark'd his face of care.

Cheer up, my son, perchance (he said)
Some tidings I may bear;
For oft when human hopes have fail'd,
Then heavenly comfort's near.

Behind yon hills so steep and high,
Down in a lowly glen,
There stands a castle fair and strong
Far from th' abode of men.

As late I chanc'd to crave an alms
About this evening hour,
Methought I heard a lady's voice,
Lamenting in the tower.

These tidings caught Sir Bertram's ear,
  He thank'd him for his tale,
And soon he hasted o'er the hills,
  And soon he reach'd the vale.

All day he sits beside the gate,
  And pipes both loud and clear;
All night he watches round the walls,
  In hopes his love to hear.

The first night, as he silent watch'd,
  All at the midnight hour,
He plainly heard his lady's voice,
  Lamenting in the tower.

The second night, the moon shone clear,
  And gilt the spangled dew,
He saw his lady through the grate,
  But 'twas a transient view.

The third night, wearied out, he slept
  Till near the morning tide,
When starting up he seiz'd his sword,
  And to the castle hey'd.

When lo! he saw a ladder of ropes
  Depending from the wall;
And o'er the moat was newly laid.
  A poplar, strong and tall.

And soon he saw his love descend,
  Wrapt in a tartan plaid;
Assisted by a sturdy youth,
  In Highland garb then clad.

Amaz'd, confounded, at the sight,
  He lay unseen and still,
And soon he saw them cross the stream,
  And mount the neighbouring hill.

Unknown, unheard of all within,
  The youthful couple fly;
But what can 'scape the lover's ken,
  Or shun his piercing eye?

With silent step he follows close
  Behind the flyingpair,
And saw her hang upon his arm,
  With fond familiar air.

Thanks, gentle youth, she often said,
  My thanks thou well hast won;
For me what whiles hast thou contriv'd,
  For me what dangers run?

And ever shall my grateful heart
  Thy services repay:
Sir Bertram could not further hear,
  But cry'd, vile traitor, stay!

Vile traitor, yield that lady up!
  And quick his sword he drew.
The stranger turn'd in sudden rage,
  And at Sir Bertram flew.

With mortal hate their vigorous arms
  Gave many a vengeful blow;
But Bertram's stronger hand prevail'd,
  And laid the stranger low.

Die, traitor, die!—a dreadful thrust
  Attends each furious word!
Ah! then fair Isabel knew his voice,
  And rush'd beneath his sword.

O stop, she cry'd; O stop thy arm
  Thou dost thy brother slay!
And here the hermit paus'd and wept,
  His tongue no more could say.

At length he cry'd, Go, lovely pair;
 How shall I tell the rest!
Ere I could stop my piercing sword,
 It fell, and stabb'd her breast.

Wert thou thyself that hapless youth?
 Ah cruel fate! they said:
The hermit wept, and so did they;
 They sigh'd; he hung his head.

My brother, alas! spake never more,
 His precious life was flown;
She kindly strove to sooth my pain,
 Regardless of her own.

Thus pouring comfort on my soul,
 Even with her latest breath,
She gave one parting fond embrace,
 And clos'd her eyes in death.

For me, I loath'd my wretched life,
 And long to end it thought;
Till time and books, and holy men,
 Had better counsels taught.

They rais'd my heart to that pure source,
 Whence heavenly comfort flows;
She taught me to despise the world,
 And calmly bear its woes.

No more the slave of human pride,
 Vain hope, and sordid care;
I meekly vow'd to spend my life
 In penitence and pray'r.

The bold Sir Bertram now no more
 Impetuous, haughty, wild;
But poor and humble Benedict,
 Now lowly, patient, mild.

My lands I gave to feed the poor,
 And sacred altars raise;
And here a lonely anchorite
 I came to end my days.

This sweet sequester'd vale I chose,
 These rocks and hanging grove;
For oft beside that murmuring stream,
 My love was wont to rove.

My noble friend approv'd my choice,
 This bless'd retreat he gave:
And here I carv'd her beauteous form,
 And scoop'd this hollow cave.

Full fifty winters, all forlorn,
 My life I've linger'd here;
And daily o'er this sculptur'd saint
 I drop the pensive tear.

The description of the hermitage shall now follow, which the reader will surely peruse with increased pleasure, connecting it in his mind with the circumstances detailed in the preceding extracts. It is probably the best preserved and most entire relic of the kind now remaining in this country. The approach is kept in neat order, but still retains its original form. A narrow walk on the brink of the river, which at this place flows without any troubled current, leads to the door of the hermitage, the walk being confined to about the width of four feet by a lofty range of perpendicular rocks on the other side. The steps, the vestibule, and the chief apartments, are hewn out of the bosom of a free-stone rock, about twenty feet high, embowered with stately trees, which impend from the top of the precipice and the fissures of the cliffs. One lower and outward apartment is of masonry. The cave contains three apartments, which have been, not unaptly, denominated the chapel, the sacristy, and the antechapel. Of these the chapel is very entire and perfect, but the two others have suffered by the falling down of the rock at the west end, by which accident a beautiful pillar, which formerly stood between these two apartments, was destroyed. The chapel is only eighteen feet long, and not more than seven and a half in width and height; but it is modelled and executed in a beautiful style of Gothic architecture. Two pilasters of semi-hexagonal form project from the opposite walls in the centre, and one from each corner, from whence spring the intersecting groins of the roof, the joinings being ornamented with roses. All the work is chiselled, and done with great mechanic regularity and exactness. At the east end there is a handsome plain altar, to which the priest ascended by two steps; these, in the course of ages, have been much worn away through the soft, yielding nature of the stone. Behind the altar is a little niche for a crucifix or image, with the remains of a glory. Perhaps the pix may have been placed here.

There is a lower apartment, constructed of masonry, the entrance to which is formed by a passage of three paces, and the door-way is marked with the remains of bolts and iron hinges. It is built up against the side of the rock, about eighteen feet square, and appears to have been the kitchen or principal dwelling, having a range or fire-place six feet wide. On the south side of this apartment, opposite to the entrance, is a door-way leading to an outward seat, formed in the rock, and opening upon the walk on the river's brink. On this side of the room are two windows which bear the marks of iron grating, and also a closet. Passing from this outward building by the same way which it was entered, a flight of seventeen steps presents itself, which conducts to a little vestibule, with a seat on each side, capable of holding one person only. Above the inner-door way some letters appear, the remains of a phrase which may be thus rendered into English: " *My tears have been my*

VOL. I.   E *food day and night."* In these seats or niches the hermit sat to contemplate, and the prospect from them was well calculated to inspire meditation. At his feet he beheld the gentle but constant lapse of the river, and its ceaseless flow might have reminded him of the unchecked current of life, which, to use the words of Young—

> Glides away like a brook,
> For ever changing, unperceiv'd the change—
> In the same brook none ever bath'd him twice;
> To the same life none ever twice awoke.
> We call the brook the same; the same we think
> Our life, though still more rapid in its flow,
> Nor mark the much irrevocably laps'd,
> And mingled with the sea.

On the south side of the altar there is another window, and below it a neat cenotaph or tomb, ornamented with three human figures elegantly cut in the rock. The principal figure represents a lady in a recumbent posture, the hands and arms of which appear to have been elevated. It is still very entire and perfect. Over her breast hovers what was probably an angel, but much defaced; this is the opinion expressed by the gentleman who communicated the account inserted in Grose's Antiquities; but Mr. Hutchinson, in his View of Northumberland, says, that "with the utmost attention, and a strong desire to coincide with others, he could not see any such figure, even with an eye prejudiced by such prepossessions; if it has ever been the representation of any figure, and now wasted by the weather beating through the windows, he conceives it was that of a child, standing in a weeping attitude over the recumbent effigies." At the feet of the lady, in a niche cut in the wall, is the figure of a hermit, on his knees, resting his head on his right hand, while his left his placed on his bosom, as if in a lamenting or pensive posture. At her feet also is a rude sculpture of a bull's or ox's head, according to Grose's correspondent, and according to Dr. Percy, in his ballad; but Mr. Hutchinson thinks that here also imagination has been set at work, and that the bull's head is nothing more than the figure of a crouching dog, placed there as an emblem of fidelity. Dr. Percy observes, that the bull's head was the crest of

The INTERIOR of

WARKWORTH HERMITAGE,

Northumberland.

Engraved by J. Greig from a Drawing by ... Stovall for the Antient Reliquaries of England & Scotland.

London Published ... for the Proprietors by Vernor & Hood, &c. &c.

the Widdrington family, whose castle is but five miles from this hermitage. It was also the ancient crest of the Nevilles, and of one or two other families in the north. Hutchinson, however, thinks it is not the crest, because its usual place on tombs is under the head of the effigies, and he cites several examples in support of his opinion. It is, indeed, more probable that the intention of the sculptor was to represent the virtues of the deceased, which was commonly done on ancient tombs by decorating them with some animal at the foot of the effigies, typical of those virtues, as a lion for fortitude, a dog for fidelity, &c.

" The west end of the chapel * is lighted by a window, formed of four conjoining circles ; above the inner door of the vestibule is a shield, bearing the remains of some arms ; by some taken to be the figure of a gauntlet ; but, as it is generally believed, one of the Bertrams formed this hermitage, so it is probable this shield (the remains of which seem to correspond therewith) bore the Bertrams arms, Or, an ore, azure.

" On the left hand of the altar, a window is formed in the partition of the apartments, divided by two mullions, the summit of each light or division ornamented with work, formed of sections of circles, like those seen in cathedrals of the tenth century. From the chapel we entered an inner apartment, by a neat door-case, over which is sculptured a shield, with the crucifixion, and several instruments of torture. At the east end of this inner apartment, is an altar like that in the chapel, lighted by the last described window, and through which the person kneeling at the inner altar could view the cenotaph in the chapel : this apartment is about five feet wide, and nine paces in length ; here is also a niche, or bason, for holy water. On the northern side of this inner chamber, a recess is cut in the rock, of size sufficient to hold the couch of a person of middling stature. I have seen several of the like form, alcoved above, and a sole about two feet above the level of the floor, to hold the mattrass and bedding of the recluse. This recess is so placed, that whilst I sat therein to make my notes, by a niche cut slantwise in the partition wall which separates the two apartments, I had a view of the cenotaph and effigies thereon.

* For this part of the description we are indebted to " Hutchinson's View of Northumberland," Vol. II. p. 275, *et seq.*

The niche seemed calculated for this very purpose; being cut through the wall aslant, it could not be conceived intended to convey the light. By some it has been imagined to be designed for confession; but it is my sentiment that the hermit was priest and penitent in one; and that he devised those apertures, that the effigies should be constantly in sight. In this inner apartment is a small closet cut in the side wall to the north; from this interior chamber is a door-way, leading to an open gallery, having a prospect up the river; but, by the falling of some of the rock above, this part is greatly damaged. It is said by old people, that the roof was supported by a fine pillar, and formed a small piazza cloister, or open gallery; such galleries are seen in very ancient mansions, in the centre of the front: one is yet perfect in the remains of Bradley-hall, in the county of Durham, the mansion of the eldest branch of the family of Bowes, built, as it is presumed, soon after the conquest.

" From these cells through a neat door-way, there are winding stairs cut in the rock, leading to its summit, supposed to conduct to the hermit's olatory, or garden. A channel is ingeniously formed on the steps to carry off the water.

" It seems evident that the original hermitage consisted of no more than the apartments hewn in the rock, the inner one being the dwelling-place, and the little cloister the summer seat, facing westward, and commanding a beautiful view up the river Coquet, which here forms a fine curve, in extent near half a mile, on this side bordered by rocks, on the other by cultivated lands, of an easy inclination; on the extremity stands a pretty farmhold, to terminate the sequestered rural prospect. The style of architecture adopted in this hermitage is of the Saxon Gothic, which proves its antiquity. In the postscript to the *poem* of the hermit of Warkworth, the author asserts, ' that the memory of the first hermit was held in such regard and veneration by the *Percy* family, that they afterwards maintained a chantry priest, to reside in the hermitage, and celebrate mass in the chapel; whose allowance, uncommonly liberal and munificent, was continued down to the dissolution of monasteries; and then the whole salary, together with the hermitage and all its dependencies, reverted back to the family; having never been endowed in mortmain.

On this account we have no record which fixes the date of the foundation, or gives any particular account of the first hermit.' The patent is extant, which was granted to the last hermit in 1532, by the sixth earl of Northumberland. The author of the poem in this postscript adds, 'After the perusal of the above patent, it will perhaps be needless to caution the reader against a mistake some have fallen into, of confounding the hermitage near Warkworth, with a chantry, founded within the town itself, by Nicholas de Farnham, bishop of Durham, in the reign of King Henry III. who appropriated the church of Branxton for the maintenance there of two Benedictine monks from Durham. That small monastic foundation is indeed called a cell by Bishop Tanner; but he must be very ignorant, who supposes that by the word cell, is necessary to be understood a hermitage; whereas it was commonly applied to any small conventual establishment, which was dependant on another. As to the chapel belonging to this endowment of Bishop Farnham, it is mentioned as in ruins in several old surveys of Queen Elizabeth's time, and its scite not far from Warkworth church is still remembered. But that there was never more than one priest maintained, at one and the same time, within the hermitage, is plainly proved (if any further proof be wanting) by the following extract from a survey of Warkworth, made in the year 1567 :—viz. Ther is in the parke also one howse hewyn within one cragge, which is called the harmitage chapel : in the same ther haith bene one preast keaped, which did such godlye services as that tyme was used and celebrated. The mantion howse ys nowe in decaye : the closes that apperteined to the said chantrie is occupied to his lordship's use.'

"It appears to me that the monks who came here in an age in which the severities of a religious life were relaxing, founded the good warm kitchen of mason-work at the foot of the rock, adapted to indulgencies unknown to the original inhabitant. The form of the doors and windows are of a much more modern mode than those above ; the windows of the hermitage have had no iron grating."

Carlisle Cathedral.

THIS venerable and stately structure was founded in a very remote period of
our history.   Pennant says, in his *first* tour in Scotland, that it was begun in
the time of William Rufus, by Walter, who was deputy of these parts, and,
it may be inferred from what is yet remaining, that the old building, when
entire, was a noble and solemn edifice.   It is now very imperfect, however,
for Cromwell violated its sanctity, and pulled down part of it to build barracks with the materials.   A strange vicissitude! Those walls that were
first erected to enshrine the peaceful but magnificent teachers and rites of
the catholic religion, were, in a subsequent generation, torn from their base
by. a usurper and a fanatic, to construct a receptacle for the sanguinary
agents of civil strife and discord.   The dilapidating hand of the artful zealot,
however, did not destroy all vestiges which could proclaim the age and character of this ancient structure.   There remains some portions of it which
were built in the Saxon times, with very massy pillars and round arches,
whose shafts are only fourteen feet. two inches high, and circumference full
seventeen and a half.   There remains also a more modern part, comparatively speaking, that which is said to have been built in the reign of Edward
III. who had an apartment in the cathedral, where he sometimes took up his
residence during his superintendence of those wars which he carried on
against the Scots.   The arches in this portion of the building are sharp-
pointed, the pillars round and clustered, and the inside of the arches taste-
fully ornamented.   Above, there are two galleries, but with windows only
in the upper; that in the east end, according to Pennant, has a magnificent
simplicity, and the painted glass displays an uncommon neatness, though
there is not a single figure upon it.

The present edifice consists of the east limb of the cross, which forms the
chancel, and the cross aisle or transept, with the tower : the greater part of
the west limb of the cross being that which Cromwell pulled down in 1641.
The architecture seems to denote an earlier era than the time of William

CARLISLE CATHEDRAL.

Cumberland.

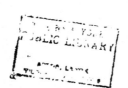

INTERIOR OF

CARLISLE CATHEDRAL.

Cumberland

Engraved by J. Greig from a Drawing by L. Clennell for the Border Antiquities of England & Scotland

London Published Sep.1.1814 for the Proprietors by Longman & Co Paternoster Row

Rufus, and though there is no corroborating evidence to establish the fact, yet it is very probable that a part of the work belongs to the age of St. Cuthbert. The west end is said to have been, in length, one hundred and thirty-five feet from the cross aisle; but only forty-three feet are now remaining. It is not easy to say how often this church has been restored, but we know that it must have happened frequently, for it is recorded in history that the Danes laid this city in ashes, and that Rufus restored it, together with the public buildings; and in the reign of Henry II. it was again laid waste by the Scots, and the public records burned. If, therefore, what we admit was probably the case, those records, as was the usual practice in those days, were deposited in the archives of the ecclesiastics, it follows that their incremation could have happened only through the burning of the place where they were kept, and consequently we must suppose that some considerable change was then produced in the external character of this sacred edifice. In 1292 it was again consumed by an accidental conflagration, which also destroyed nearly one half of the city as far as the north gate. In the reign of Edward III. it was rebuilt by contributions, and the editor of Camden says, " Almost in the middle of the city stands the cathedral church; *the upper part* whereof (being newer) is a curious piece of workmanship, *built by king Henry VIII.* but the lower is much more ancient. The lower west part is the parochial church, and as old as St. Cuthbert; or as Walter, who came in with the Conqueror, was a commander in his army, rebuilt the city, founded a priory, and turning religious, became himself the first prior of it. The chancel was built by contributions, about the year 1350, and the belfrey was raised, and the bells placed in it, at the charge of William de Strickland, bishop in the year 1401." There is some obscurity in this account, which antiquaries have not been able to elucidate. It is sufficiently evident that the destruction of this cathedral at any time could only have been partial, if the observation of Pennant be true, that some of its architectural remains are of Saxon origin.

The following brief but adequate description of its late state and condition is given by Hutchinson, in the second volume of his *Antiquities of Cumberland.*

" The choir is one hundred and thirty-seven feet in length, and with the side aisles, seventy-one feet broad; the cross aisle, or transept, is twenty-eight feet broad, so that the length of the church, when entire, was exactly three hundred feet within. The choir is of fine Gothic architecture, with

light columns, remarkably beautiful.   The stalls are garnished with taber-
nacle work; (the organ is placed at the cross screen, which contains but a
narrow and low entrance, and is a great injury to this fine edifice.)   By
late repairs it is greatly embellished, being wainscotted with oak, from the
stalls round the whole east end of the choir, in a simple style, after the
old order.   The open gates leading into the side aisles are old and much
broken, but shew excellent light tracery work, finely ornamented.   The
bishop's throne is not magnificent, but yet elegant and stately.   The breadth
of the choir and aisles being seventy-one feet, corresponds well with the
height, which to the centre of the ceiling is seventy-five feet.   The roof was
originally lined or vaulted with wood, painted and ornamented with arms
and devices of the several patrons and contributers to the work; with the
arms of France and England were those of the Piercys, Lucys, Warrens,
and Mowbrays.   The old wood lining remains in the cross aisle, and shews
what was the former figure, and the ornaments of the choir: but the outward roof and wood ceiling of the choir having gone greatly to decay, when
repairs were made, in 1764, the ceiling was stuccoed, in the form of a
groined vault, which is a great advantage to its appearance.   The east
window is large, being forty-eight feet in height, and thirty in breadth,
ornamented with fine pilasters; but it has no cast of solemnity, by means of
a border of coloured glass thrown round it, of yellow, red, and green, which
looks gaudy."*

In the aisles on each side, observes Pennant, in his *Second* Tour in Scotland, are some strange legendary paintings of St. Anthony, St. Cuthbert,
and St. Augustine: one represents the saint visited by an unclean spirit,
who tempts him, in a most indecent manner, as these lines import:

The spyrit of Fornication to him doth aper;
And thus he chastineth hys body with thorne and with bryer.

* " The official duties of marriages, christenings, churchings, and funerals, are performed in
the parish church; the ordinary duties of the Sabbath, and prayers twice a day through the
year, in the choir.   On the burial of any of the members of the choir, the corpse is carried into
that part of the church.   The cathedral and parish church are both under one roof.   It has a
stately steeple, with a ring of eight bells, which are rung on all public occasions.   The consis-
tory, or spiritual court, is kept in part of the church.   In the abbey, contiguous to the church,
and in which properly the church stands, are several venerable buildings, such as the deanery,
fratery, head-school, cloisters, porter's-lodge, &c."

CARLISLE CASTLE,
Cumberland [?]

Engraved by J. Shury, from a drawing by S.J. Davies, for the Border Antiquities of England & Scotland.

Carlisle Castle.

THERE are few cities in England which have been the scenes of more momentous or more interesting events than Carlisle. During those years when the borders of the two countries were the theatre of the alternate triumph and defeat of both, it shared, with suffering fidelity, in the fierce contests of its warlike possessors: and even at a later period, when rebellion reared her bloody standard in the north, Carlisle was at once the witness of crime and the scene of its punishment. Recently, also, the muse of a popular writer has excited an increased interest concerning all that relates to border transactions; and among those transactions where will one be found, of any importance, that is not more or less connected with Carlisle and its towers of defence? The office of warden of the marshes was one commonly bestowed upon nobles of tried fidelity and known courage: and in their train were to be found the youthful aspirers after military glory, who longed to signalize themselves in feats of arms, where bravery was opposed to bravery, and the wreath of glory was won, not by a single achievement or by desultory prowess, but by continued watchfulness, labour, and skill.

In modern times, since law has held its mild dominion instead of the ferocious and turbulent supremacy of arms, Carlisle castle has lost much of its importance and much of its utility. It is now regarded rather as a venerable relic of antiquity than as an edifice formed for defence; and yet the mind feels a sentiment of sober and solemn delight in recalling the occurrences which are connected with it through every period of English history. In reference also to the peculiar plan of this work, it assumes a feature of individual attraction, and a brief but accurate sketch of its past and present condition shall now be given.

It was founded, according to Pennant (Second Tour in Scotland), by

William Rufus, who restored the city after it had lain two hundred years in ruins, to which state it had been reduced by the barbarous outrages of the Danes. Richard III. made some additions to it; and Henry VIII. built the citadel, an oblong with three round bastions, seated on the west of the town: in the inner gate of this castle is still remaining the old portcullis; and here are shewn the apartments of Mary Queen of Scots, where she was lodged for some time after her landing at Workington; and where, after being for a short period entertained with flattering but insidious respect, she found herself the prisoner of her jealous and implacable rival.

A tolerably correct notion of the ancient state of Carlisle castle may be formed from the following report of its condition in the reign of Queen Elizabeth; it is a curious document, and will be read with interest by those whose love of antiquarian knowledge impels them to accuracy of research.

"First, the dungeon tower of the castle, which should be principal part and defence thereof, and of the town also, on three sides is in decay, that is to say, on the east and west sides in length 66 feet, and on the south side 66 feet in decay; and every of the same places so in decay, do contain in thickness 12 feet, and in height 50 feet; so as the same dungeon tower is not only unserviceable, but also in daily danger to fall and to overthrow the rest of the said tower.

Item, there is a breach in the wall in the outerward, containing in length $69\frac{1}{2}$ feet, in thickness nine feet, and in height with the battlement 18 feet, through which breach men may easily pass and repass.

Item, the Captain's tower, another principal defence, wanteth a platform, and the vawmer about 44 feet, in breadth 40 feet, and in thickness eight feet.

Item, three parts of the walls of the inner ward is not vawmer; containing in length 344 feet, and in thickness 12 feet, and in height three feet, with one half round.

Item, the castle gates are in decay, and needful to be made new.

Item, there is not in the said castle any store-house meet for the ordnance and ammunition, so as the same lieth in the town very dangerously for any sudden enterprize.

CARLISLE CASTLE.

Cumberland.

Pl. 2

Engraved by J. Greig from a Drawing by J. Schnebbelie for Scottish Antiquities or Peeps at Scotland

London Published Feb.1 1824 for the Proprietors by Longman & Co Paternoster Row

Engraved by J. Greig, from a Drawing by L. Clennell, for the Border Antiquities of England & Scotland.

CARLISLE CASTLE,

Cumberland

Pl 3.

London Published Feb 1.1814 for the Proprietors by Longman & Co. Paternoster Row.

Item, there is decayed the glass of two great windows, the one in the great chamber, and the other in the hall of the said castle.

IN THE CASTLE : sagars two ; fawcons four, all dismounted ; fawconets two, whereof one not good ; one little pot gun of brass ; demi-bombarders two ; balls double and single ; 12 lacking furniture ; half-stags 39, not serviceable ; bows of ewe none ; arrows six score, sheafs in decay ; morrispikes 30, not good ; sagar-shot of iron 58 ; sagar-shot of lead 70.

There is a breach in the town wall between the castle and Rickardgates, containing in length 40 feet, and in height with the battlement 18 feet, falling down in such decay that men may easily pass and repass through the same ; and at either end of the said breach 40 feet of the same wall is in danger of falling, and very needful to be repaired from the foundation.

Item, on the east part of the city is 120 feet of the vawmer in decay.

Item, there is a great part of the vawmer of the new wall unfinished, containing in length 400 feet, and in height six feet.

Item, there is in the same wall near unto Caldergate 36 feet in decay, and very needful to be repaired.

Item, one half round tower called Springold-tower, being chief and principal piece and defence of two parts of the city, and helping to the castle, unserviceable, and very needful to be repaired.

Item, the vawmering of Calder-tower is in decay, and it is very needful to have a platform thereon.

Item, it it needful that Rickardgate have a new roof and be covered with lead, and thereupon a platform, being a meet place for service.

Item, the gates of the city being of wood are in decay, and one broken, which are to be repaired with celerity.

Fawcons of brass five, all dismounted ; fawconets of brass four, dismounted ; one small pot-gun of brass. Fawcons of iron two, dismounted also, to serve the wardons in the field. Fowlers two, small serpentine two, bases two, all lacking their furniture. Hagbuts 13, whereof 12 unserviceable ; harquebuses 36, decayed and past service. Bows of yew 12, bows of elm 70, not serviceable ; sheaves of arrows 18, in decay. Serpentine powder one last and a half, both for the city and the castle ; being all placed in the city because there is no ordnance-house in the castle : corned powder one demi-barrel and a half.   Hacks and picks 52, worn and decayed with work ; shovels and spades 10 dozen ; quarrel-picks 12 ; cast furniture for 30 horse draught.   Hemp rope two coil, small.   Sagar short of iron 50 ; fawcon shot of iron 50 ; one quarrel mill.   Waller's hammers 40 ; setting chisels nine ; hand-baskets 10 dozen ; gavelocks five ; iron 12 stone.   Lanterns 20, in decay.

The great round tower at the east end of the fort of the citadel being paved with stone and sand upon the lead roof, was thereby so overcharged as that a great part thereof is fallen to the ground, and is very needful to be repaired ; for that it is the principal of that fort, and standeth upon the most danger of the town.

Item, there be two houses within the said fort, called the battery and the boulting-house, standing within the rampier wall, the roofs and timber whereof are fallen to the ground, by means of the like being overcharged with earth, so as the same are both unserviceable.

Item, it is needful to have a platform upon the old Gatehouse-tower, being a requisite place of service.

Item, another platform were needful upon the half-round tower towards the town.

Item, there is the glass of a great window in the hall of the said fort utterly decayed, by means of a great thunder and hail-stones.

Sagars two, fawcons four of brass, dismounted ; double-bases three, single bases eight ; small serpentines two ; fowlers two ; murderers two, all unfurnished ; harquebusses nine, not serviceable : half-haggs 14 decayed and past service ; morrispicks 40, not good ; corned powder two demi-barrels, whereof four of the grained sort.   Bows of yew 20, not good ; arrows 26 sheaves in decay ; sagar shot of iron 50."*

The above singular enumeration may possibly suggest to the reader a curious question, whether our ancestors were exactly those faultless beings which their posterity are so apt to consider them ? We find here a castle of

* Brit. Musæ.

the utmost importance as a place of warlike defence, so admirably provided that it was no defence at all: nothing in it, scarcely, but unserviceable stores.

That the castle of Carlisle, though suffered to be thus inadequately supplied with warlike provisions, was a place of much importance, need not be particularly urged: but there is a passage in the Memoirs of Robert Cary, Earl of Monmouth, one of Queen Elizabeth's favourites, exceedingly curious, and as it is connected with the present subject it may not be unacceptable to the reader. Cary went to Carlisle as the deputy to Lord Scroope, who was appointed governor of the castle, and warden of the West Marches.

"Thus," says he, "after I had passed my best time in court, and got little, I betook myself to the country, after I was passed one and thirty years old, where I lived with great content, for we had a striving world, and few days passed over my head but I was on horseback, either to prevent mischief or to take malefactors, and to bring the border in better quiet than it had been in times passed. God blessed me in all my actions, and I cannot remember that I undertook any thing in the time I was there but it took good effect. One memorable thing of God's mercy shewed unto me was such as I have good cause still to remember it.

" I had private intelligence given me that there were two Scottishmen that had killed a churchman in Scotland, and were, by one of the Greenes,* relieved. This Greene dwelt within five miles of Carlisle; he had a pretty house, and close by it a strong tower for his own defence in time of need. I thought to surprise the Scots on a sudden, and about two o'clock in the morning I took horse in Carlisle, and not above 25 in my company, thinking to surprise the house on a sudden. Before I could surround the house the two Scots were gotten into the strong tower, and I might see a boy riding from the house as fast as his horse could carry him, I little suspecting what it meant. But Thomas Carleton came to me presently, and told me that if I did not presently prevent it, both myself and all my company would be

* It should be Græmes, a powerful clan of borderers, of whom some account may be found in a note on the Lay of the Last Minstrel.

either slain or taken prisoners. It was strange to me to hear this language. He then said to me, 'Do you see that boy that rideth away so fast? He will be in Scotland within this half hour, and he is gone to let them know that you are here, and to what end you are come, and the small number you have with you; and that if they will make haste, on a sudden they may surprise us and do with us what they please.' Hereupon we took advice what was best to be done. We sent notice presently to all parts to raise the country, and to come to us with all the speed they could; and withal we sent to Carlisle to raise the townsmen; for without foot we could do no good against the tower. There we staid some hours expecting more company; and within short time after the country came in on all sides, so that we were quickly between three and four hundred horse; and after some little longer stay the foot of Carlisle came to us to the number of three or four hundred men, whom we set presently at work to get up to the top of the tower, and to uncover the roof; and then some twenty of them to fall down together, and by that means to win the tower. The Scots seeing their present danger offered to parley, and yielded themselves to my mercy. They had no sooner opened the iron gate and yielded themselves my prisoners, but we might see four hundred horse within a quarter of a mile coming to their rescue, and to surprise me and my small company; but of a sudden they staid, and stood at gaze. Then had I more to do than ever, for all our borderers came crying with full mouths, 'Sir, give us leave to set upon them; for these are they that have killed our fathers, our brothers, our uncles, our cousins; and they are come thinking to surprise you upon weak grass nags,* such as they could get on a sudden; and God hath put them into your hands, that we may take revenge of them, for much blood that they have spilt of ours.' I desired they would be a patient awhile, and bethought myself, if I should give them their wills, there would be few, or none of them (the Scots) that would escape unkilled (there were so many deadly feuds among them), and therefore I resolved with myself, to give them a fair answer, but not to give them their desire. So I told them, that if I were

* Horses taken up from grass and unfit for hard exercise.

not there myself, they might then do what pleased themselves; but being present, if I should give them leave, the blood that should be spilt that day would lie very heavy upon my conscience, and therefore I desired them, for my sake, to forbear; and if the Scots did not presently make away with all the speed they could, upon my sending to them, they should then have their wills to do what they pleased. They were ill satisfied with my answer, but durst not disobey. I sent with speed to the Scots, and bade them pack away with all the speed they could, for if they staid the messenger's return, they should few of them return to their own home. They made no stay; but they were returned homewards before the messenger had made an end of his message. Thus, by God's mercy, I escaped a great danger; and, by my means, there were a great many men's lives saved that day."

When it is remembered that the citadel was built, according to Pennant, by Henry VIII. it may justly excite our wonder that it should have fallen into so much decay as it appears to have been in when the report was made to Queen Elizabeth: but, though neither Pennant, nor Hutchinson, in his History of Cumberland, has suggested any reason for this, it may probably have arisen from the fact, that King James, when he found neither threats nor vapouring made any impression upon Elizabeth, adopted the milder course of forbearance and silence; and so early as 1587 he prohibited the incursions on England, and this was met by a similar prohibition on the part of Elizabeth with respect to Scotland. In that state of suspended hostility, if not of sincere amity, Carlisle castle ceased to be of so much importance as a military possession; and hence, probably, its dilapidated state and insufficiency in stores as described in the report.

To present here a concentrated statement of that report, it may be observed, that the works consisted of a dungeon, whose walls are twelve feet in thickness; an inward and outward ward; the walls of the outward ward nine feet in thickness and eighteen feet in height; and the walls of the inner ward twelve feet, having a half-moon bastion. A tower called the Captain's tower. Two gates, one to each ward. In the castle a great chamber and a hall, but no storehouse for ammunition. In the walls of the town, three gateway towers, a semi-circular bastion, called Springhold tower; and to these may be added the citadel. But besides those mentioned in the report, the walls were garnished with several square towers, particularly a tower at the western sallyport, and another called the Tile tower, of particular strength.

The scenery, as exhibited from the elevated site of this castle, is described by all travellers with great admiration; Pennant dwells with much complacency upon it, and Mr. Hutchinson describes it as follows: "The foreground is formed of level meads washed by the Eden; in one part insulated by a separation of the river. This plot is ornamented by two fine stone bridges; one of four, the other of nine arches, the great passage towards Scotland. The hanging banks are crowned with the village and church of Stanwix, and the distant ground filled with the mountains of Bewcaste. To the south you command the plains towards Penrith, shut in on either hand by a vast chain of mountains, over which Crossfell and Skiddaw are distinctly seen greatly eminent. To the east, a varied tract of cultivated country, scattered over with villages and hamlets, mingling beautifully with woodlands on the extensive landscape; the distant horizon formed by the heights of Northumberland. To the west, the Frith spreads out its shining expanse of waters, margined on this hand by a cultivated tract; on the other by the Scotch coast, where Creffel and a chain of mountains extend towards the ocean."

In the rebellion of 1745, Carlisle castle, together with the town, fell into the hands of the rebels, but was recovered by the Duke of Cumberland, and its walls were disfigured by the dismembered limbs of those who had espoused the hopeless cause of Prince Charles. It may not, perhaps, be unacceptable, for it will certainly relieve and adorn the arid nature of antiquarian discussion, to conclude this account with the following beautiful stanzas written by a nameless bard, and deploring, in language singularly plaintive and expressive, the sufferings of his hapless countrymen in that ill-fated enterprize. The strain has been collected from oral tradition by one whose genuine love of the Scottish muse was unquestioned: it unites pleasingly with the present topic, and its perusal cannot but give delight abstracted from all relative considerations.

Engraved by Edwd Finden from a Drawing by H. Gastineau for the Patriae Antiquities of Scotland & Ireland

CARLISLE YETTS.

White was the rose in his gay bonnet,
As he faulded me in his broached plaidie
His hand whilt clasped the truth of luve,
O it was ay in battle readie!
His lang lang hair in yellow hanks
Waved o'er his cheeks sae sweet and ruddie;
But now they wave o'er Carlisle yetts
In dripping ringlets clotting bloodie.

My father's blood's in that flower tap,
My brother's in that hare bell's blossom;
This white rose was steeped in my luve's blood,
An' I'll ay wear it in my bosom.

When I first cam by merry Carlisle,
Was ne'er a town sae sweetly seeming;
The white rose flaunted o'er the wall,
The thistled banners far were streaming!
When I cam next by merry Carlisle,
O sad sad seem'd the town an' eerie!
The auld auld men came out and wept—
'O maiden come ye to seek yere dearie?'

There's ae drap of bluid atween my breasts,
An' twa in my links o' hair sae yellow:
The tane I'll ne'er wash, an' the tither ne'er kame,
But I'll sit and pray aneath the willow.
Wae wae upon that cruel heart,
Wae wae upon that hand sae bludie,
Which feasts in our richest Scottish bluid,
An' makes sae mony a doleful widow!

It is but a fragment: yet nature speaks in her most eloquent strain through every line.

G

𝕷𝖆𝖓𝖊𝖗𝖈𝖔𝖘𝖙 𝕻𝖗𝖎𝖔𝖗𝖞.

IN CUMBERLAND.

THE remains of this venerable structure still excite the attention of the traveller, and the investigation of the antiquary. They are situated in a vale of singular beauty and amenity, where the eye reposes with placid delight upon the tender and elegant beauties of a picturesque landscape, while softened and quiet features seemed to lull every worldly care to rest, and to open the heart and mind to the admission of solemn, pensive, and endearing images. Combined with these charms, thus freely scattered by the lavish hand of nature, stand the sacred ruins of Lanercost Priory, and by recalling the purposes to which the building was formerly applied, the imagination at once connects the past and present, the actual view with the intellectual retrospect, and peopling the valley with the inhabitants of former times, those inhabitants whom fiction, with a laudable violation of truth, still loves to regard as beings above the vulgar turmoil and the vulgar pleasures of this life, places a picture before its contemplation which possesses more than the sober charms of truth, and purifies the heart by reminding it of the virtues of solitude and retirement. Perhaps there would be few studies more liable to degenerate into futility than antiquarian research, if it were unconnected with those moral sentiments which the aspect of ruins is so calculated to produce; but when, like the philosophic duke of Shakspeare, we can

> Find tongues in trees, books in the running brooks,
> Sermons in stones, and good in every thing,

then the pursuit becomes ennobled by the object to which it is made sub-servient. No man is to be envied for his feelings, who can look unmoved

LANERCOST PRIORY,
Cumberland.

London, Published Apr.1 1811 for the Proprietors, by Longman & Co. Paternoster Row.

Engraved by J. Scott from a Painting by L. Clennell for the Border Antiquities of England & Scotland

INTERIOR of

LANERCOST PRIORY,

Cumberland.

London Published Oct. 1.1814 for the Proprietors, by Longman & Co. Paternoster Row.

upon the mouldering remains of pure consecrated buildings, or some embattled edifice: who can behold the ruined heap, and not heave a sigh over
the perishable qualities of all human greatness!

Something analogous to what the traveller on classic ground experiences,
he who beholds the finest remains of ancient architecture converted by the
present degraded possessors of Greece into the vilest instruments of domestic use, may be felt by him, though in a subdued degree perhaps, who
visits the priory of Lanercost. He will there find some parts of the monastic
buildings converted into a farm-house, and others so perverted from their
original purpose as to leave few traces of what the whole has been. It has
been ascertained, however, that the chief part of the monastery was repaired
in the sixteenth century, for the neat mansion of one of the Dacres; and the
old stately projecting window of the convent is still visible. Part of the
cemetery grounds has been converted into gardens, and several stone coffins
and inscribed monuments lie among the trees. In reading this, who does
not remember the natural and philosophic interrogatory of Young?

Where is the dust that has not been alive?

The church is built in the form of a cross, and the gateway consists of a
circular arch of many members, richly ornamented and supported on pilasters, the capitals and bases of which are without any other embellishment
than plain rolls. There is a statue of Mary Magdalen in a niche above
the entrance, which is of excellent workmanship. It is in stone; and
though it has not escaped the ravaging hand of time, yet enough remains
to shew that the drapery of the figure was most elegantly disposed. On
the right hand there is a diminutive figure of a kneeling monk. The canopy
of the niche is circular, and is supported on pilasters which are ornamented
with the heads of cherubs. This part of the edifice has been recently
repaired, and made fit for the performance of divine service. It is the
parochial church of the parish of Lanercost, and is capable of containing a
great many people.

There is, on the right of the communion-table, a tablet fixed in the wall,
on which is the following inscription:

"Robertus de Vallibus filius Hubert. Dns de Gillsland, fundator priorat. de Lanercost A'. dni. 1116. Ædargan Uxor ejus sine prole."

The import of this is, that Robert de Vallibus, son of Lord Gilsland, founded the priory in 1116, Edargyne his wife having no issue. There is another inscription in the great window above the communion-table, which runs thus:

> Mille et quingentos ad quinquaginta novemq.
> Adjice, et hoc anno, condidit istud opus;
> Thomas Daker, Eques, sedem qui prim. in istam,
> Venerat, extincta religione loci.
> Hec Edvardus ei dederat, devoverat ante
> Henricus longe præmia militiæ.
> Anno Dni. 1559.

This inscription is said to have been removed from the window of the hall, which is now used as a barn. The walls of the other parts of the church, and the centre tower, are still standing, but they are unroofed.

We shall now proceed to a description of the edifice, both as it appears at present, and as far as induction will carry us, as it formerly was.

"The cross aisle* is thirty-two paces in length, and the quire twenty-six. The triner has formed a spacious cupola, each corner supported by a clustered pillar, light and well proportioned. An open gallery or colonnade runs round the upper part of the whole edifice, supported on single pillars without any dead space or interval—a circumstance uncommon in such buildings, and which gives a light and beautiful appearance to this. The arches of the gallery are pointed, but the principal ones of the building are circular; though most of the windows are lancet under pointed arches. The tower is low and heavy, without ornament, except an embrazoned battlement. The ceiling of the cupola is of wood work, but retains no escutcheons of arms, or other decorations. The quire is lighted to the east, by three long lancet windows below, and an equal number above, and two windows on each side. The whole structure is plain, of excellent masonry,

* See Hutchinson's Cumberland, i. 54.

INTERIOR OF

LANERCOST PRIORY.

Cumberland.

WEST FRONT OF

LANERCOST PRIORY,

Cumberland.

London. Published Nov. 1 1814, for the Proprietors, by Longman & Co. Paternoster Row.

and constructed of a durable stone. At each end of the cross aisle are several tombs, richly sculptured with the arms of the Howards and Dacres; from their exposure the inscriptions are obliterated, the ornaments defaced, and the whole grown green with moss. The veneration for ancestors in former ages was an incitement to practical virtues; we lament to see any thing which should tend to promote good works sinking into neglect. These monuments are shamefully forgotten, now overgrown with weeds, and not so much veneration is paid to the remains they cover as to preserve them from rapacious hands, or their resting-place from reptiles, vermin, and loathsome filthiness.

"We were told by an old person who lived near the abbey, that some years ago one of these sepulchral vaults fell in, which excited his curiosity to see the remains deposited there, when he found several bodies entire; one in particular, with a white beard down to his waist: but the air in a few days reduced them to dust."

According to the tablet in the church, this was a monastery of the order of St. Augustine, and founded in 1116: but no mention of it in the records occurs earlier than the 16th year of Henry II. 1169. Its endowments consisted of all the lands lying between the *Picts' Wall and Irthing*, and also between Burgh and Poltross, and several other valuable possessions. Bernard, bishop of Carlisle, dedicated the church to Mary Magdalen. The several grants that had been made to the priory, were confirmed by charter of Richard I. and several similar confirmatory charters were made by Henry III. and Edward I. The latter monarch granted to the prior and convent the advowson of two churches in his patronage, because the priory had been burnt, and the lands ravaged by an incursion of the Scots. He wrote an epistle to the pope expressly to obtain his sanction to this grant, which was not withheld. Many other liberal donations were made to this monastery, and some of them exhibited the peculiar character of the times, such as the tithes of venison and the skins of deer and foxes: tithe of the mulcture of a mill, pasture for milking and sheep, the bark of trees, a well or spring, and sundry villeins their issue and goods.

No account has been discovered of the succession of priors, beyond the year 1360.

The arms of this monastery, according to Tanner in his *Notitia*, were a *flasque or & gules*. At the time of the suppression, there were a prior and seven canons here: the revenue 77*l*. 7*s*. 11*d*. according to Dugdale, and 79*l*. 19*s*. according to Speed. The site of the religious house, as well as many of the adjacent lands, were then granted to Thomas Dacre, in the 34 Henry VIII. at that time deemed the patron, as being the lineal descendant of the founder, and heir, to Robert de Vallibus. He held these lands of the king *in capite*, to him and his heirs lawfully begotten for ever, by the service of the twentieth part of one knight's fee and nine shillings sterling rent. The male line failing, the lands and site of the priory are now in the tenure of the Earl of Carlisle, who holds a court baron and customary court.

Lanercost is at present no more than a perpetual curacy, and was certified to the governors of Queen Anne's bounty at 14*l*. 5*s*.: it has received one allotment of 200*l*. The Earl of Carlisle is patron.

Two curious inscriptions have been discovered at Lanercost, and were communicated by George Smith, Esquire, to the Gentleman's Magazine. (See vol. xiv. p. 369.)

Bothwell Castle,

NORTHUMBERLAND.

This dilapidated structure stands in the midst of beautiful and picturesque scenery, which harmonises finely with its venerable remains. Bold promontories and rocky precipices mingle with hanging woods, and verdant vales, stretched forth in a variety of windings, contrast their amenity with the rude and rugged elevations that overhang them. On one of those eminences stand the ruins of Bothwell Castle, and, though thus built, it may be considered as seated in a deep valley, so mountainous is the scenery by which it is surrounded.

The relics of this mansion consist, at present, chiefly of the great gateway, which is flanked on the north side by two polygonal towers, each of them fifty-three feet in height: and on the south-west angle by a square turret, measuring sixty feet in height. The outward wall extends, from the towers of this gate, along the brink of the eminence, in a circular form, enclosing the area and interior buildings of the castle. Within this enclosure about half an acre is contained, over which space are scattered some fragments of the inner buildings, but in so mutilated a state that it is not possible to conjecture what was their original form, or what their use. There was formerly another tower to the north-west of the gateway, which was called Ogle's tower, and was pulled down during the last century. To the south, the site of the castle is very lofty, being on the bring of a rock, the foot of which is washed by the river; but the east and west sides, as more accessible, were defended by a moat.

The gateway of the castle and its towers bear indubitable evidence of being the most modern part of the structure. The outward gate was defended by a portcullis, and there are three square apertures in the arching of the gateway, through which the garrison could successfully annoy any assailants who might happen to have gained the first gate. There is on each side a door which conducts to the flanking towers. The passage and stair-case to the south-west tower is on the right-hand, and at the foot of the stairs the door opens, which leads to the prison. Imagination can hardly conceive any place more gloomy and horrible than those dungeons in baro-nial castles which were allotted for the incarceration of captives: but here some guiding spirit of benevolence seemed to actuate the architect, for the prison, instead of being excavated from the dark recesses of the earth, was above ground; the cheerful light of heaven was admitted to gladden the sight of the forlorn inhabitant, though gleaming only through the narrow apertures of massy walls, and the fanning breeze might sometimes breathe upon his wan and faded cheek, finding its passage through the same channel. Yet even this was comfort compared to the damp, dark, and profound cell, which commonly served for the dwelling of those whom the chance of war, or crime, or perfidy, placed within the power of the rude, unfeeling, and ferocious owners of these embattled edifices.

Opposite to the stairs that lead to the prison, and on the opposite side of the gateway, is a large hall; and above the gateway is the state-room. This is lighted by four windows, but neither of them are of any considerable size. The centre and principal one faces the north. The hugh walls of this castle allowed space for benching the recess formed for the window with stone seats for six persons at least. The view from this window embraces the town, the church, and a narrow vale through which the river flows. There is a door on each side, which leads to the flanking towers. The fire-place, a spacious one, is to the east; and on the left side of it there is another win-dow with a recess, with stone benches for the accommodation of persons, like the one just described; and, to the right of the door as you enter there is a third window, similar to the two former, which looks into the area of the castle. To the west there is a large window, which commands the under part of the vale, and the fine hanging woods by which it is bounded. Three large stones cover the apertures in the floor which open upon the passage of the gateway. The upper rooms are in a more ruinous state, and, conse-quently, cannot be so easily described, nor their form or uses so precisely

BOTHALL CASTLE,
Northumberland.

Pl. 2.

Engraved by J. Greig from a Drawing by E. Dayell for the Border Antiquities of England & Scotland.

ascertained. In the front of the gateway are several shields of arms, arranged, according to Hutchinson (*View of Northumberland, Vol. II. p. 307*), in the following order, and which, he thinks, correctly designate the period when this part of the castle was built.

" In the centre, in a large shield, are the arms of England and France quarterly. It is observable that England takes the first quarter, a thing I have never observed an instance of before. On the dexter side, a shield with the arms of *England, three lions passant gardant;* on the sinister, a shield with the arms of the Grays, *barry of six argent and azure, three torteauxes in chiefe.* This denotes that the erection was made in the time of Edward IV. whose consort was a Gray, mother of Thomas Gray, who in the 15th year of that reign, was created Marquis of Dorset. Beneath, in the centre, the arms of Bertram, *Or, an orl, azure.* On the dexter and sinister sides of this are three shields, which denote the alliances of the Bertram family.

" The first, on the dexter side, the arms of Percy.

" The second of Dacre.

" The third of Vesey, Or, a cross, sable.

" The first, on the sinister side, of Darcy.

" The second of Hastings.

" The third, two lions passant gardant in a tressure; but to what family this coat armour appertains I cannot form any probable assertion.

" On the tower on the right hand of the gateway are four shields, the chief of which is of the Ogles; but as they are greatly defaced by time, and on my view did not seem to have any material relation to the date or history of this erection, I passed them without particular attention: but on considering the matter, I am induced to believe that John Ogle, the grandson of the heiress of Bertram, erected this gateway. In the family of Ogles, afterwards mentioned, he is particularly noticed. In the centre, on the battlements, is the figure of a man, in stone, in the attitude of sounding a horn; on the right-hand tower is another figure, holding a ball between his hands: these figures are greatly injured by the weather."

The barony of Bothwell belonged for several centuries to the family of the

H

Ogles, a race of great antiquity in the county of Northumberland, where they possessed an extensive property before they succeeded to the Bothwell estate by intermarriage. Cuthbert, the seventh and last lord Ogle, had two daughters, Johanna and Catherine. The latter married Charles Cavendish of Welbeck in Nottinghamshire. She was created Baroness Ogle. Her son, Sir William Cavendish, was advanced to successive dignities in the peerage by James I. Charles I. and Charles II. As the Marquis of Newcastle he distinguished himself by his adherence to his royal master during the civil wars. His loyalty, however, was fatal to him; he was compelled to fly the country; his extensive estates were sequestered; some of them were sold; and he, with six others, were exempted from the general pardon. At the restoration he was reinstated in his possessions, and, having an only daughter, she married John Hollis Duke of Newcastle, who in her right became possessed of the castle of Bothwell. His only daughter married Edward, Earl of Oxford and Mortimer. These possessions devolved on *their only* daughter Lady Margaret Cavendish Harley, who married the Duke of Portland, in which family they now remain.

WARKWORTH CASTLE.

Northumberland.

Bamborough Castle,

———

OF this important and interesting structure, interesting from its present application to the noblest purposes of charity, a brief and general character shall first be given in the words of Pennant, and then, such particulars added as are requisite in a work like the present.

"On an eminence on the sea-coast, about four miles from Belford, is the very ancient castle of Bamborough, founded by Ida, first king of the Northumbrians, A. D. 548. It was called by the Saxons Bebbanburh,* in honour of Bebba, Ida's queen. It was at first surrounded with a wooden fence, and afterwards with a wall. It had been of great strength; the hill it is founded on is excessively steep on all sides, and accessible only by flights of steps on the south-east. The ruins are still considerable, but many of them now filled with sand, caught up by the winds which rage here with great violence, and carried to very distant places. The remains of a great hall are very singular; it had been warmed by two fire-places of a vast size, and from the top of every window runs a flue, like that of a chimney, which reached the summits of the battlements. These flues seem designed as so many supernumerary chimneys, to give vent to the smoke that the immense fires of those hospitable times filled the rooms with: halls smoky, but filled with good cheer, were in those days thought no inconvenience. Thus my brave countryman Howel ap Rys, when his enemies had fired his house about his ears, told his people to rise and defend themselves like men: '*For shame, for he had knowne there as greate a smoake in that hall upon a Christmas even.*'†

* Saxon Chr. 19.

† This historical, and truly characteristic fact, has been employed by Sir Walter Scott in his last poem of Rokeby. Redmond, rallying the domestics to make head against the banditti, exclaims,

Engraven by I. Daney from a Drawing by L. Clennell for the Border Antiquities of England and Scotland.

BAMBOROUGH CASTLE,

Northumberland. Pl. 2.

London, Published Nov. 1 1814 for the Proprietors by Longman & Co Paternoster Row.

Engraved by Craig from a Painting by H Weber for the Border Antiquities of England & Scotland.

along this tempestuous coast for above eight miles, the length of the manor, by which means numbers of lives have been preserved. Many poor wretches are often found on the shore in a state of insensibility; but by timely relief are soon brought to themselves.

"It often happens, that ships strike in such a manner on the rocks as to be capable of relief, in case numbers of people could be suddenly assembled: for that purpose a cannon is fixed on the top of the tower, which is fired once, if the accident happens in such a quarter; twice, if in another; and thrice, if in such a place. By these signals the country people are directed to the spot they are to fly to; and by this means frequently preserve not only the crew, but even the vessel; for machines of different kinds are always in readiness to heave ships out of their perilous situation.

"In a word, all the schemes of this worthy trustee * have a humane and useful tendency: he seems as if selected from his brethren for the same purposes as Spenser tells us the first of his seven beadsmen in the house of holinesse was.

> "'The first of them, that eldest was and best,
> Of all the house had charge and government,
> As guardian and steward of the rest;
> His office was to give entertainment
> And lodgings unto all that came and went:
> Not unto such as could him feast againe
> And doubly quit for that he on them spent;
> But such as want of harbour did constraine;
> Those, for God's sake, his dewty was to entertaine.'"

Thus far Pennant, who has, naturally, dwelt upon those topics which interest every reader, rather than upon those, which peculiar inclination and study must qualify us for enjoying.

Part of the most ancient fortifications of this castle, on the land side, are broken and defaced by the falling of the cliffs on which they were erected. A circular tower remains on this side, of very antique construction, its

* The Rev. Thomas Sharpe, B.D.

base projecting several tiers. The gateway is placed on the only accessible part of the rock; it was defended by a deep ditch cut through a narrow neck communicating with the main land, having a drawbridge. It is strengthened by a round tower on each side: and about twelve paces distant you approach a second and machicolated gate, of more modern architecture, and provided with a portcullis. Beyond this second gate, on the left hand, stands a very ancient round tower. It is of great strength, built on the lofty point of the rock, and commands the pass. This part of the fortress is probably of Saxon origin; though Grose and some others ascribe the whole of the buildings to the Norman period.

It is admitted, by all writers, that Bamborough is of great antiquity, and was a fortress of singular consequence and strength in the early times of the Saxons. Many memorable events in history are connected with this castle. It was repeatedly besieged, pillaged, and redeemed at successive periods. At the time of the Conquest it was said to be in good repair, when it was probably entrusted to the custody of some faithful Norman, who made additions to the works, for the present area contained within its walls measures upwards of eight acres instead of three as described by Hoveden. In the border feuds, Bamborough castle was repeatedly the scene of contentions. If the reader wishes for a minute account of its various history, he may consult Hutchinson's Northumberland, vol. ii. p. 158 et seq.

Pennant, in the account already quoted, has hinted at the possession which the Forsters once held of this castle, and how that possession was forfeited by a descendant of the family in the rebellion of 1715, the castle and manor belonging to it being then purchased by Lord Crew, who by his will, dated the 24th June, 1720,* devoted it to purposes of the most extensive practical benevolence that ever issued from the hands of a private individual in any country. That all seamen may be informed of the circumstances of this charity, a printed account is published under the direction of the Trinity-house in Newcastle-upon-Tyne, containing ample

---

* His lordship died on the 18th September following, in the 88th year of his age.

directions for signals both on shore and at sea, a statement of the assistance, stores, and provisions prepared for shipwrecked mariners, and rewards specified for those who are most active in giving notice of vessels in distress, or assisting their crews. It is to be regretted that no similar plan has been adopted on the southern coast of England, by which many acts of barbarity might be prevented, and many valuable lives saved to the public.

In regard to natural strength, there is not a situation in all Northumberland equal to Bamborough, or one so admirably adapted to the ancient rules of fortification.

Wetherall Priory.

This religious edifice, founded for monks of the Benedictine order, is seated on the western banks of the river Eden. The surrounding scenery is rich and beautiful, as may be anticipated; for it is one of the invariable characteristics of these religious abodes (and the only proof of good taste which their founders or possessors have left to posterity) that the spots chosen for their site were rich in all the lavish adornments of nature. It is the same in all parts of Europe. Some of the most lovely scenes the writer of this article ever beheld were those he contemplated in Spain from the cells or gardens of nunneries and monasteries; and if any thing could have tempted him to a life of seclusion and silence, it would have been the opportunity afforded him by these retreats, for conversing with his Creator in meditating upon the most endearing works of his hand.

What was left of this edifice by the zealots of Henry VIII.'s reign was demolished (except the gateway, or lodge, with a fine elliptic arch, which is now converted into a hay-loft) by the Dean and Chapter of Carlisle, who built a prebendal house, &c. in Carlisle with the materials. The gateway is of plain architecture, and does not require description. Wetherall was an inferior house, a cell to the abbey of St. Mary's in York. It was founded by Ranulph de Meschines in the year 1088 for a prior and eight Benedictine monks, and was dedicated to the Holy Trinity, St. Mary, and St. Constantine; it was given, together with the church, mill, fishery, wood, and the chapel of Warwick, with two bovates of land in Corby, to the abbey of St. Mary's. King William Rufus confirmed to the abbey of St. Mary's what Meschines had granted, and added the whole pasture between Eden and the King's highway, which leads from Carlisle to Appleby, and from Wetherall to Drybeck. All these grants were further confirmed by Henry I. who gave to the priory pannage for swine in his forest, without

WETHERAL PRIORY,
Cumberland.

Engraved by W. Gray from a Drawing by J. Donald for the Border Antiquities of England & Scotland.

London, Published Jan.ry 1, 1813 for the Proprietors by Longman & Co. Paternoster Row.

paying the usual forest dues for the same. Soon after its foundation it was richly endowed, having many benefactors. In the year 1650 the manor of Wetherall, and all the possessions of the Dean and Chapter there, were sold by the commissioners of Oliver Cromwell to Richard Banks of Cockermouth, for 1044*l*. 5*s*. 1*d*. On King Charles's restoration, restitution was made to the Dean and Chapter.

Tynemouth Priory.

THIS edifice is situated in Northumberland, and lies to the east end of the town of Tynemouth. It stands on a peninsula formed of stupendous rocks on the north side of the mouth of the river Tyne. The approach to the priory is from the west, by a gateway tower of a square form, with a circular exploratory turret on each corner: from this gateway a strong double wall extended on each side to the rocks on the sea-shore, which, from their rugged shape and great height, were considered as inaccessible. The whole was defended by a deep ditch, with a drawbridge over it. The tower comprises an exterior and interior gateway, the former having two gates about six feet apart, the inner of which is defended by a portcullis and an open gallery; the latter, or interior, is likewise defended by a double gate. The area between the gateways is a square of about six paces, and open above, so that those on the top might annoy any assailants who had gained the first gate. Various accounts prove that this was a place of great strength in very remote antiquity. What it was in the Saxon period there is little evidence to decide. Its situation on the *ostium* of so important a river induced William the Conqueror to convert it into a strong hold. As such it shortly after took the name of Tynemouth Castle, and belonged to the Earls of Northumberland for several generations. Peck, in his *Desiderata Curiosa*, mentions it among the bulwarks and fortresses that were garrisoned in Queen Elizabeth's reign. Camden speaking of it, says, " it is now called Tynemouth Castle, and glories in a stately and strong castle." During the civil wars it was besieged by the Scots (in 1644), when it surrendered to the Parliamentarian army. Parliament appropriated a large sum to repair the injuries it had sustained during the siege, and Colonel Henry Lilburn was made governor of it; but he deserting his party, the garrison soon after revolted. Sir Arthur Hazelrig, who lay at Newcastle,

PART OF

TYNEMOUTH MONASTERY,

Northumberland.

Engraved by Sidney Hall & Published by E. Tomkell for the Beauties of England & Scotland and Wales.

Engraved by T. Grieg from a Drawing by L. Clennell, for the Border Antiquities of England and Scotland.

PART OF
TYNEMOUTH MONASTERY,
Northumberland.

London Published Nov. 1, 1814, for the Proprietors by Longman & Co. Paternoster Row.

marched immediately to reduce them, and took the place by storm, in which the most intrepid bravery was displayed by the assailants; they scaled the walls at the very mouths of the cannon, and entered by the embrazures and port-holes: they soon became masters of the fortress, and Lilburn was slain in the conflict.

On passing this gateway the view is crowded with august ruins, which impress the spectator with a melancholy sense of the grandeur that once prevailed, where now only an unsightly heap of dilapidated walls presents itself. These ruins are so disunited, that it is impossible to determine their relation to any particular part of the structure when it was entire. Those which appear in front as you enter the gateway are probably the remains of the cloister. After passing this gate many modern tombs appear in the area, for this ground is still used as a place of sepulture. The west gate entering into the abbey is still entire. The ground from the cloister to the south wall is almost covered with the foundations of buildings, which are probably the remains of the priory. Two walls of the east end of the church are standing; the end wall to the east contains three long windows; the centre window is the loftiest, being near 20 feet high, and is richly ornamented with mouldings; some of rose work, and others of the *dancette*, as the figure is termed in heraldry, or zig-zag, a decoration common to old Saxon architecture.

The divisions or pillars between the windows are enriched with pilasters of five members, embellished with highly finished foliated capitals and cornices. There is an oval one with like mouldings over the centre window, and on each side there are the openings of a gallery. Part of the south side wall of the choir is also standing, illuminated with four windows similar in shape to those on the east, and though not of equal altitude yet ornamented in the same way; the arches in the windows of this part are circular, the blank arches, which are thrown upon the wall beneath the windows, are pointed. There is a remarkable lightness and beauty predominant in the architecture of the whole of this part of the building.

There is a doorway beneath the centre window, at the east end, of excellent workmanship, and which leads to a small but elegant apartment, which, it is thought, contained the shrine and tomb of St. Oswine. A human head appears on each side of the door, carved in a style much superior to the general taste of the age to which they are ascribed. The apartment is nine feet in breadth and height, and eighteen feet in length. On the south side is an entrance from the open yard with two windows; three windows on the north; and a circular one to the east. This last is so elevated as to allow room for an altar beneath it: at the east end there are two niches for statues, a closet for the vessels appropriated to sacred offices, and a bason for holy water. There is the figure of a kneeling monk on each side of the window, and two of the emblematical animals commonly depicted with the evangelists: the side walls are ornamented with pilasters, from whence spring the groins and arches of stone which in various intersections form the roof: the joinings are enriched with circles of carved work, and the interstices of the roofs are arched and constructed with thin bricks. Each of the circles contain sculptures of the divine personages with the apostles. There is a circular belt round each sculpture, with a sentence in the old English character well raised, viz. *Sanct. Petrus. ora P. nobis, &c.* The centre row consists of four circles, in one of which are the effigies of St. John the baptist, with a similar sentence; in a second (toward the west) are effigies of our Saviour, with a kneeling monk; in a third to the east, the effigies of the supreme, with a lamb bearing an ensign; and in the fourth, a representation of the last judgment, with this sentence, *In die judicii liberare nos.* Above the door are the effigies of our Saviour with a globe in his hand: at the bottom are these words, *Morit P. nobis.*

There are two escutcheons, the dexter one charged with bearings of Vesey, a cross sable: the sinister, the bearings of Brabant and Lacy, quarterly. On the outside, at the east end, are two coats of armour supported by cherubs.

The time when this monastery was first founded, as well as the founder, are both equally uncertain. But though it be impossible to ascertain the exact era of its foundation, there are ample proofs of its antiquity, which reaches to a period earlier than the eighth century. Many great personages lie interred here; and there have been, of this house, several learned men. Malcolm, king of Scotland, and his son Edward, slain near Alnwick, 1094, are both buried here; and John de Tynemouth, an eminent biographer, was born here. He flourished about the year 1366.

The annual revenues of this monastery, unconnected with St. Albans, were, at the dissolution, valued by Dugdale at 396*l*. 10*s*. 5*d*.; by Speed at 511*l*. 4*s*. 1*d*.

The site of the priory, in the 5th year of King Edward VI. was granted to John Dudley, Duke of Northumberland, but on his attainder it reverted to the crown, and remained ungranted till the 10th year of Queen Elizabeth. (See Tanner's Notitia.)

The *manor of Tynemouth* is now part of the possessions of his grace the Duke of Northumberland.

Much of the remains of this priory was pulled down by Mr. Villars for erecting the barracks, light-house, his own house near it, and other edifices: he likewise stripped off the lead which, till then, had covered the church.

Jedburgh Abbey,

ROXBURGHSHIRE.

THE Abbey of Jedburgh is situated in Teviotdale, on the west side of the river Jed, near where it empties itself into the Teviot. In a charter granted by Willlam the Lyon, of Scotland, to the abbot and monks of Jedburgh in the year 1165, the names of Jedwarth and Jedburgh are promiscuously used; but in modern times the appellation of Jedburgh is alone retained. It was sometimes, however, written with a G; and is supposed to be derived from the Gadeni, a tribe which anciently possessed the whole tract lying between Northumberland and the river Teviot.

The abbey was founded by King David I. for canons regular, who were brought from the abbey of St. Quintins, at Bevais, in France. It is now partly in ruins, while that which is entire serves as the parish-church. The architecture and workmanship are very superior. Many of the arches are circular, and seem of great antiquity.

There were two cells belonging to this abbey at Restenote and Canonby. Restenote is in Angus-shire, a mile to the north of Forfar, and is encompassed with a loch, except at one passage where it had a drawbridge. It was here that all the papers and other valuable things belonging to Jedburgh were kept. In 1296, Robert, prior of this house, swore fealty to Edward I. who, at that time was suspicious of the intentions of John, King of Scotland, and marched northward with numerous forces to chastise his rebellious vassal.

The priory of Canonby is situated on the river Esk, in Eskdale, and shire of Roxburgh. Neither tradition nor record has preserved any memorial of the precise period of its foundation: but it is probable that we may date it antecedent to 1296, in which year William, prior of this convent, also

SOUTH EAST VIEW of

JEDBURGH ABBEY.

Roxburghshire

Drawn & Engraved by S. Sparrow for the Border Antiquities of England & Scotland

London Published April 1st 1814, for the Proprietors, by Longman & Co. Paternoster Row.

Engraved by J⁰ Craig from a Painting by G⁰ Arnald A.R.A. for the Border Antiquities of England and Scotland.

THE WEST FRONT OF
JEDBURGH ABBEY CHURCH ROXBURGHSHIRE.

London Published May 1ˢᵗ 1813. for the Proprietors by Longman & C⁰ Paternoster Row.

NEWTON ABBEY.

Harburghshire.

Engraved by J. Sharp, from a Sketch by J. Smith A.R.S.A. for the Border Antiquities of England & Scotland.

PL.3

London, Published Nov 1814 for the Proprietors by Longman & Hurst ...

Engraved by Sidney Hem a Painting by A. Smith L.L.L. in the Scottish Antiquaries in England & Scotland

swore fealty to Edward I. In those ages of fierce contest between the borderers, religious houses, the known repositories of wealth, were frequently plundered and destroyed; this was more than once the fate of Canonby priory, and its peaceful inhabitants, driven from their cloisters and cells of meditation, were but little able to preserve an unbroken series of their records. Hence it becomes almost impossible to give an accurate account of them.

Of Jedburgh, however, Fordun mentions the following abbots.

Osbert, the first abbot, who died A. D. 1174. He was succeeded by Richard Cellarer, of that house.

A. D. 1249, the abbot Philip died, and was succeeded by Robert de Giseburn.

A. D. 1275, abbot Nicholas being superannuated, he abdicated the pastoral staff. He is recorded as a wise and provident man, though nothing is told of what he did to merit those epithets. His substitute was John Morel, a canon of the house; and which terminates the little that inquiry has been able to collect respecting either his predecessors or successors.

We may learn from Bede, l. iv. c. 27. and l. v. c. 12. that Roxburghshire was, in the age of Cuthbert, and long afterwards, a part of Northumberland. It became, therefore, the scene of many a sudden inroad, and many a desperate conflict, according to the varying issue of which it was incorporated with England or with Scotland. These continued incursions and sanguinary frays materially affected the welfare of Jedburgh abbey, so that in process of time neither the condition of the house nor its funds were adequate to the lodging and maintenance of the canons. Edward I. who, in the midst of conquest, forgot not the interests of religion, as they were then considered, sent several of these canons to different religious houses of the same order in England, that they might be there maintained till this house could be repaired and restored to better circumstances. There is still extant a writ, by which a canon, named Ingelram de Colonia, was sent to the convent of Bridlington, in Yorkshire.

Keith, in his Appendix to the History of the Church and State of Scotland, estimates the revenues of this house, according to the surplus books, in which, however, are annexed the dependent priories of Restenote and Canonby, at 1274*l.* 10*s.* in money. The books of the collectors of the thirds and that of assumption make the money 974*l.* 10*s.*; but the difference arises probably from the omission of the two dependent priories in the latter.

This abbacy was erected into a temporal lordship in favour of Sir Andrew Ker of Ferneherst, ancestor to the Marquis of Lothian. He was high in favour with King James, on account of his learning and great parts. He made him one of the gentleman of his privy-chamber in 1591, and afterwards raised him to the dignity of the peerage by the title of Lord Jedburgh, his patent being dated the 2d February, 1622.

NEWARK CASTLE,

Selkirkshire.

Newark Castle,

SELKIRKSHIRE.

THIS castle was built as a hunting seat, by James the Second, a monarch whom Drummond of Hawthornden describes as " endowed with what conditions and qualities are to be desired or wished in a king, both for mind and body." The royal arms, with the unicorn, are engraven on a stone in the western side of the tower. In the immediate vicinity of this edifice there stood a much more ancient castle, called Auldwark, which was founded, according to some accounts, by Alexander III. Both of them, however, were erected with a view to gratify regal pleasure; for their proximity to the extensive forest of Ettricke, which in ancient times was a royal chace, and abounded with all sorts of game, made them frequently the resort of the Scottish monarchs, when they partook of the toils and sports of hunting.

In the records of the privy-seal there are various grants, bestowing the keeping of Newark castle upon different barons. There exists also a popular tradition that this defence was once seized and kept by the outlaw Murray, a noted character in song, and who only surrendered it upon condition of being made hereditary sheriff of the forest. This tradition has been made the subject of a long ballad, which may be read in the first volume of the Border Minstrelsy.

When James IV. who perished with the flower of his nobility at the disastrous battle of Flodden, espoused Margaret, the sister of Henry VIII. the castle of Newark, with the whole forest of Ettricke, was assigned to her as part of her jointure lands. But they proved of little benefit to her when he who had granted them was gone; for after the death of James,

K

she complained heavily that Buccleugh had seized upon them. The office
of keeper, indeed, was latterly held by the family of Buccleugh, and with
so firm a grasp, that when the forest of Ettricke was disparked they
obtained a grant of the castle of Newark in perpetuity.

The court-yard of this castle was the scene of that sanguinary vengeance
which the parliamentarian General, Lesly, wreaked upon the Scotch royalists
under Montrose, after the battle of Philliphaugh. This battle was fought
on the 13th September, 1645. Philliphaugh is but a few miles from Selkirk.
The conflict was obstinately contested; and Hume says that Montrose was
surprised. But from a manuscript account in the Advocate's Library, and
from another that was published by the victors, under authority, at London,
immediately after the battle, it appears that the parliamentarian army was
greatly superior in numbers. The covenanters used the victory with much
severity. Besides several persons of distinction who went through the
mockery of a trial and were executed, no less than 100 of the captives
were shot at a post in the yard of Newark castle.

The Buccleugh family for more than a century made this an occasional
seat; and here Anne, the first Duchess of Monmouth and Buccleugh, was
born. During the minority of the present Duke of Buccleugh, the castle
was partly destroyed: the wooden beams and such stones as could be removed being employed in building a miserable farm-house in the vicinity.

The noble proprietor very justly regretted this violation of antiquity, when
he came to years that qualified him to judge of its character; for, with some
appropriate additions and repairs, the old tower might have been converted
into a noble and stately mansion.

The form of this castle is that of a massive square tower. It is now unroofed, and in a state of entire decay. It is surrounded by an outward
wall, and defended by round, flanking turrets. The circumjacent scenery
is highly picturesque. The castle is situated on the banks of the Yarrow,
a fierce and precipitous stream, which unites with the Ettricke about
a mile beneath the castle. A fine back ground is formed by Newark
hill, which rises at a little distance, and adds greatly to the effect of the
landscape.

Engraved by J.Greig, from a Painting by L.Clennell, for the Border Antiquities of England & Scotland

The INTERIOR of
NEWARK CASTLE.
Selkirkshire.

London Published May 1.1814 for the Proprietors by Longman & Co. Paternoster Row.

It may be mentioned among the local peculiarities of this spot, that the brother and mother of Mungo Park occupy the farm of Foulshiels in the neighbourhood. It was also the abode of that celebrated traveller himself for some months previous to his leaving England upon his last, and fatal undertaking.

Bothwell Castle,

CLYDESDALE.

THE castle of Bothwell is a very ancient and noble structure. " Tradition
and history," says Pennant, " are silent about the founder." Though in
a state of decay, it exhibits striking features of its former magnificence,
and may be reckoned perhaps the most splendid ruin in Scotland. It is
constructed of a polished red stone, and the apartments are exceedingly
lofty. What remains of it occupies a space in length of 234 feet, and in
breadth of 99 feet over the walls. The lodgings are confined to the east
and west ends, and many of them sufficiently distinguished. The chapel
is marked with a number of small windows, and off from it there is like a
chamber of state, with two large windows to the south. The old well in
the corner of one of the towers, penetrating through the rock to a good
spring, was discovered a few years since. The stair of one of the highest
towers is entire almost to the top, and reaches to an exceeding height
above the river. The court in the middle was probably designed to contain
the cattle and provisions in case of an assault, an arrangement peculiar
to many ancient castles. The entry is on the north, about the middle of
the wall; and vestiges of the fosse are still visible. It seems to have
received successive additional enlargements from its several proprietors.

The earliest mention that is made of Bothwell is in a writ bearing date
1270, by which certain mulctures are remitted to the monks of Dryburgh.
We have already stated that tradition has preserved no record of its
founder: but the lords of Bothwell occupy a distinguished place in Scottish
history. Among these, Sir Andrew de Moravia, Dominus de Bothwell,
deserves to be mentioned as one of the first, who leagued himself with
Wallace in the sacred cause of defending his country's liberties and
freedom. He was slain at Stirling in 1297; but his virtues and his name

BOTHWELL CASTLE,

Clydesdale.

Engraved for this Work exclusively by J. Johnson, as to North Antiquities of England & Scotland.

descended to his son, who emulated the patriotism of his sire, and assisted
Bruce in defending his claim to the crown. That claim was finally established after innumerable wars; and the fidelity of Bothwell was rewarded
by the hand of the sister of Bruce. After the disastrous battle of Bannockburn, disastrous to the invaders—glorious to the invaded, Bothwell castle
became the refuge of many of the English nobility, who sought within its
walls safety and protection from the avenging swords of a people fighting
for independence. Bruce attacked the fugitives in their strong hold, and
soon reduced them to capitulation. The fortune of war, however, again
transferred it to the English, and Edward III. took up his residence here,
and published writs, dated from this castle, ordering his parliament to
assemble; but in the next year (1337), the Earl of March and Sir William
Douglas obliged it to submit to the army under their command.

It has been observed of this castle, that it "hath often given the title of
Earl, but never lasted long in a family, and hath been generally unfortunate,
so that no one now enjoys that title." Major, the Scottish historian, says,
that the castle of Bothwell was *levelled to the ground* in 1337: upon which
assertion Pennant pertinently remarks, that it "seems a favourite phrase
of the historian; for to me it appears to be in the same state with that of
Caerlaveroc, and was only dismantled; for in both, some of the remaining
towers have all the marks of the early style of building."

The following is a concise statement of the various lords or masters
whom it acknowledged according to the vicissitudes of fortune:

"It was anciently possessed by the Murrays; but in the time of King
Edward I. it was given to Aymer de Valance, Earl of Pembroke, governor
for him of the south part of Scotland. Upon his forfeiture, it was given by
King Robert Bruce to Andrew Murray, Lord Bothwell, who married
Christian, sister to that king. With his grand-daughter it came to Archibald
the Grim, Earl of Douglas, by marriage, and continued in their family till
their forfeiture by King James II. 1455. After the forfeiture of the family
of Douglas, the bulk of the lordship of Bothwell was given to Lord Crighton, son to Chancellor Crighton; and Bothwell forest, or Bothwell moor,
was given to Lord Hamilton, in exchange of the lands of Kingswell.

"Crighton was forfeited in 1485, for joining with Alexander, Duke of Albany, against King James III. It was then given by King James III. to the Lord Monipenny, from whom it was soon retaken, as having been given by the king in his minority; and was thereafter given by him to John Ramsay, his favourite, who enjoyed it till the year 1488, when he was forfeited for counterfeiting a commission under the great seal to the Earl of Northumberland; then the lordship of Crighton was gifted by King James IV. to Adam Hepburn, Lord Hailes, whom he created Earl of Bothwell. It continued in his line till November 1567, when James, Earl of Bothwell, was forfeited for the murder of Henry, father to King James VI. Thereafter it was given by that king to Francis Stewart, son of John abbot of Kelso, who was natural son to King James V. and he being forfeited for crimes committed against James VI. his estates were gifted to the Lairds of Buccleugh and Roxburgh, from whom the Marquis of Hamilton acquired all the superiority and patronage of that lordship.

"The property, which was less than the third of the lordship, with the castle of Bothwell, having been disponed by Hepburn, Earl of Bothwell, to the Earl of Angus, in exchange of the lordship of Liddisdale,

"The said William, Earl of Angus, and Archibald his son, in 1680, or thereby, did sell the third part of the lordship to the particular servants and possessors thereof, without diminution of the old rent, and reserving the castle and mains of Bothwell. It was given off as a patrimonial portion with the Earl of Forfar, but is again returned to the family of Douglas, by the death of Archibald, Earl of Forfar, who died at Stirling of his wounds received at Sherriff-muir in the year 1715."

A superstitious mind might fancy it beheld a fatality in the possession of this castle and title, which seemed to entail upon their owners inevitable perfidy and disloyalty. The succession of proprietors is rendered credible, however, by this circumstance, that the different parts of the edifice retained, each, the name of the builder, such as *Valence* tower, *Douglas* tower, *Hamilton* tower, and the *Cuming* tower; and some are still known by them. The Douglas family had exceedingly enlarged and improved it; their arms were found in different parts of the wall. It is impossible to form a just idea of its former greatness, as it is said that much of it was taken down by the Earl of Forfar, out of which he built a modern house. The present possessor, also, Archibald, lord Douglas, has built an elegant modern mansion, near the castle, of the red stone peculiar to the country, and the same as that of which the castle is constructed. His lordship has likewise formed beautiful walks on the banks of the river. In the drawing-room are several good portraits of the Douglas family.

There is one peculiarity attached to this superb structure: all the surrounding objects partake, more or less, of grandeur and sublimity. The Clyde makes a fine circle round the castle; the breadth of the river is considerable; the banks on both sides are very high, and adorned with natural wood. The craig of Blantyre, with the ruins of the priory upon the top of it, being immediately opposite, has a striking effect: while this noble monument of ancient grandeur, extending along the summit of the north bank, with a bold aspect to the south, rears its lofty towers at both ends, and dignifies the whole scene.

From Bothwell castle, in 1645, the gallant but unfortunate Marquis of Montrose dated his *protection*, August 28, 1645, to the learned and ingenious Drummond of Hawthornden, by which all the officers and soldiers serving under him were prohibited from molesting the lands or tenantry of that accomplished person. (See Drummond's Works, fol. Edit. Edin. 1711, p. 157.)

Mitford Castle and Church,

NORTHUMBERLAND.

THE ancient castle of Mitford is now a rude heap of ruins, situated on a considerable natural eminence. It is defended towards the north and west by a deep ditch, and on the south the river Wansbeck washes the foot of the castle hill: the works appear to cover about an acre of ground. Of this fortress the principal part consisted of a *circular tower* raised upon an artificial mount, the chief elevation from the natural level being produced by stone arches and vaults, which, in ancient times, were employed as prisons, or places for concealment. The tower was defended by an outward wall, which ran parallel to it, and at the distance of about ten feet. The prospect from this eminence is very circumscribed; the vale is so enclosed on all sides by hills. It is impossible to trace, or even to conjecture, what other buildings or apartments may have been erected within these walls; their present ruinous state forbids all speculation. The origin of this building is involved in equal obscurity: it is supposed to have been erected before the conquest, but neither its date nor its first owner is known.

At the period of the conquest, however, it is ascertained that Sir John Mitford was in possession of this castle, and his only daughter and heiress, Sibille, was given in marriage by the Conqueror to Sir Richard Bertram, a Norman knight, by whom he had two sons, William and Roger. The Bertrams of Mitford were afterwards persons of much property and distinction in this county.

William succeeded to the manor and castle of Mitford, and it was created a barónage by the grant of King Henry I. His son Roger, desirous of adding greater improvements to Mitford, paid a fine of fifty marks to King Henry II. for a weekly market at his town of Mitford.

Roger Bertram, a lineal descendant, having joined with the northern

MITFORD CASTLE,

Northumberland.

Engraved for Grose's view in Britain by Sparrow, for the Rerde Antiquities in England & Wales

London Published by Hooper & Wigstead

MITFORD CASTLE,

Northumberland Pl. 2

Engraved for Tubing Phils...... by J. Greville for the Border Antiquities of England & Scotland

barons in the 17th year of King John, that detested tyrant, ferocious because weak, and cruel because pusillanimous, marched from Dover to Berwick, with foreign mercenaries in his train, and devastating in his course the provinces on each side of him. The barons of the north had rendered themselves peculiarly obnoxious to this perfidious monarch, both because they were the first to rouse the nation in defence of its liberties, and because they openly expressed their discontent even at the concessions contained in the Great Charter. He hastened therefore with his *Rutars*,* or Flemish troops, to inflict signal vengeance on them. He seized on this castle, and destroyed the town of Mitford with fire and sword. The barons, with their families, fled into Scotland, and offered allegiance to Alexander, who, in the ensuing year, besieged the castle, but whether he took it is not mentioned.

Philip de Ulcotes was the person upon whom the crown bestowed the barony of Mitford, thus forfeited: but upon the king's demise, Bertram propitiated his successor Henry III., and for a fine of 100*l.* obtained a restitution of his lands. Nor was this all: he acquired so much of that monarch's esteem and confidence, that he obtained permission, on the payment of ten marks, to hold his annual fair at Mitford for eight days instead of four. His successor, Roger Bertram, was one of the insurgents at Northampton against Henry III. where he was taken prisoner, his estates confiscated, and the castle given by Edward I. to Eleanor Stanour, wife of Robert de Stoteville.

In 1316 this castle was in the possession of a noted freebooter, called Gilbert Middleton. Stowe relates, that after many injuries done to the

---

* So called, according to some, from the Teutonic or German word *Rotte* (not *Rot*, as Gibson writes in his Camden,) which signifies, when applied to troops, a file of them. But it also denotes a rude, lawless rabble, or gang; and when it is remembered for what purpose these mercenaries were introduced, also how they conducted themselves, it seems more consistent to derive the appellation from that interpretation of the term. Gibson adds, that *Rottiren* signifies a muster in the German language: but there again he errs, for it denotes *to complot, to conspire;* (see Radlein, and Fahreünkrger,) and this signification of the derivative strengthens ours of the primitive word *Rotte*, and the corrupt one *Rutars.—M.*

L

priory of Tynemouth, and other places, he was at length taken in his castle by Ralph Lord Greystock and others, and carried to London, where he was executed. Two years afterwards (1318) Alexander, king of Scotland, took it, dismantled it, and destroyed most of its fortifications.

The entire barony of Mitford then became the property of Adomer de Valence, Earl of Pembroke. It appears from the escheats of the 17th Edward II. that this castle was then in ruins, having been destroyed by the Scots.

"This earl," says Hutchinson, "seemed to have a divine interdict impending over him, and the immediate vindictive hand of Providence to be upon him and his posterity for his atrocious deeds. He was a tool to his prince, and servilely submitted to the mandates of the crown, contrary to the dictates of humanity, honour, and justice. He sat in judgment on Thomas Earl of Lancaster, and impiously acquiesced in his sentence. He was a chief instrument in apprehending the famous Scotch patriot Wallace of Craiggy in 1305, accomplishing his capture by corrupting his bosom friends, and by the treachery of his most intimate associates, and those in whom he placed his utmost confidence, Sir John Monteith, and others of infamous memory. *Adomer* on his bridal day was slain at a tournament, held in honour of his nuptials, and left a wife at once a *maiden, bride,* and *widow.* It is said, that for several generations of this family *a father was never happy enough to see his son;* the proscribed parent being snatched off by the hand of death before the birth of his issue."

The Earl of Athol afterwards became possessed of this barony by Johanna his wife, of the Pembroke family, from whom, by female heirs, it passed to the Percys. It then came, by two coheiresses, into the families of Brough and Gray; and it appears from Leland, that in the reign of Henry VIII. the castle and manor were in the possession of Lord Brough. In the 4th year of Queen Mary, Lord Brough granted these possessions to Cuthbert Mitford and Robert his son for ever, a collateral branch of the ancient owner before the conquest, reserving the site of the castle and royalties. These came afterwards to the crown, and were granted to the abovemen-

Engraved by J. Irving from a Drawing by L. Ginnell as in the Border Antiquities of England & Scotland

REMAINS of the

MITFORD CHURCH.

Northumberland

Engraved by J.Greig from a Painting by J.Stewart for the Beauties of England & Wales

London, Published April 1, 1812 by the Proprietors, by Vernor & Hood, Poultry

Engraved by J. Storer from a Painting by L. Clennell, for the New Series of England and Scotland.

SOUTH DOOR

MITFORD CHURCH,

Northumberland.

London, Published May 1st, 1816, by Sherwood, Neely & Jones, Paternoster Row.

tioned Robert Mitford in the reign of Charles II., to whose descendants the estate now belongs.

The church of Mitford, with the impropriation and advowson, was granted by King Edward I. to Lanercost priory in Cumberland. There is a tomb in this church, with a rude effigy of one of the Bertrams, the inscription dated 7th October, 1622.

Holyrood Abbey.

THOUGH it has been customary with most writers who have described this building to blend their account of it with the palace of Holyrood, we shall endeavour to neglect a custom certainly more " honoured in the breach than the observance," and present to our readers a distinct relation of those particulars which specifically belong to the abbey.

Its foundation is correctly ascribed to David I. A. D. 1128, who erected it for canons regular of St. Augustine. According to Arnot, (see his History of Edinburgh) he bestowed on these canons the church of Edinburgh castle, and those of St. Cuthbert's, Corstorphine, and Liberton in the county of Mid-Lothian, and of Airth in Stirlingshire. The priories of St. Mary's isle in Galway, of Blantire, in Clydesdale, of Rowardill in Ross, and of Crusay, Oransay, and Colunsay, in the Western Isles, also belonged to them : the canons received from King David, likewise, the privilege of erecting a borough between the town of Edinburgh and the church of Holyrood-house, which still retains the name of Canongate,* with a right to hold markets in it. He also gave them portions of land in different parts, with a most extensive jurisdiction, and right of trial by duel, and fire and water ordeal. Certain revenues were allotted them, which were payable out of the Exchequer and other funds ; with fishing, and the privilege of erecting mills on the water of Leith. These mills, from the nature of the individuals in whom the privilege was originally vested, are still called the Canon Mills.

Nor were these the only acts of royal munificence, directed by the impulse of pious bigotry, bestowed upon this foundation. Succeeding sovereigns emulated each other in heaping immunities, grants, and revenues upon

* Holyrood abbey and palace stand at the bottom of the street called Canongate, formerly the residence of the nobility; now the meanest street in the old town of Edinburgh.

INTERIOR OF THE

CHAPEL OF HOLYROOD.

Edinburgh.

Engraved by J. Craig, from a Painting by L. Donnell for the Border Antiquities of England & Scotland.

INTERIOR OF

HOLYROOD CHAPEL,

(W. End)

London Published Mar. 1 1815, for the Proprietors by Longman & Co. Pater noster Row.

olyrood abbey, so that it soon became one of the most opulent religious tablishments in Scotland. Its annual revenues at the time of the reformaon were estimated at 442 bolls of wheat, 640 bolls of bear, 560 bolls of ts, 500 capons, two dozen of hens, two dozen of salmon, twelve loads of lt, besides a number of swine, and about two hundred and fifty pounds erling in money.

The church of Holyrood-house suffered considerably when the English urned down the palace, at the time of their invasion by sea, in the year 544; but the dilapidations were soon repaired, and the wasteful fury of ar left no vestige to record its barbarities. Kincaid, in his Appendix, No. 25.) has collected several curious particulars respecting this event. ccording to him, nothing was left standing but the body of the church, hich was a magnificent Gothic structure. The brazen font belonging to was carried off by Sir Richard Lea, captain of the English pioneers, who resented it to the church of St. Albans, in Hertfordshire, having caused to e engraved on it the following haughty and imperious inscription:—

" When Leith, a town of good account in Scotland,
And Edinburgh, the principal city of that nation, was on fire,
Sir Richard Lea, knight, saved me out of the flames, and brought me into England.
In gratitude to him for his kindness,
I, who heretofore served only at the baptism of the children of kings,
Do now most willingly offer the same service even to the meanest of the English nation:
Lea, the conqueror, hath so commanded. Adieu!
A. D. 1543, in the 36th year of King Henry VIII."

No doubt this mighty hero, who had achieved so glorious an enterprise s that of taking away a brass font in the midst of the tumult occasioned y a conflagration, hoped to inform posterity of his renown by the memoial engraven on the trophy won by his exploits: but, alas! ambition knows ot its own destiny. The victor's spoil became, in its turn, the spoil of ebellious regicides; for during the civil wars that raged under the unforunate Charles, this sacred emblem of conquest was taken down, sold for its veight, and ignobly destroyed: nor would the memory of Sir Richard Lea's alour have survived but for the diligence of an accurate antiquarian.

Three years subsequent to the burning of part of this edifice the English committed further ravages upon it. In 1547, after the battle of Musselburgh, they uncovered the roof of the church, and conveyed away the lead and the bells. When Charles the Second was restored, among the other things which he did to testify his veneration for his ancestors (though his negligent efforts to discover his father's burial-place deserve the severest censure), was the rebuilding the palace of Holyrood, and completely repairing the church; after which he ordered that it should be set apart as a chapel royal in all future time, and not employed as the parish-church of the Canongate, which it had hitherto been. It was accordingly fitted up in a very elegant manner; a throne was erected for the sovereign, and twelve stalls for the knights of the order of the thistle. A regal act of munificence, in return for the *devoted loyalty* which the Scotch had shewn to his father in the hour of persecution and sorrow. It happened unfortunately, however, that this chapel royal was decorated with an organ: an instrument of abomination to Presbyterian apprehension, and of sounds most unholy to Presbyterian ears. To this crime was added another, that of mass having been celebrated there in the reign of James VII. At the revolution, therefore, the people exhibited another proof of their attachment to the race of Stuart, by despoiling the church of all its internal decorations, and leaving nothing but the bare walls. Fanatical fury and political apostacy went further. They violated the sacred habitations of the dead; they profaned the sepulchre of their kings; they outraged its sanctity by tearing open the coffins that held the mouldering ashes of James V.; of Magdalen of France, his first queen; of the Earl of Darnley, once their monarch; and of others who had held the Scottish sceptre. Avarice maintained divided empire with religion over their minds. They sold the lead of which the coffins were made, and left the bodies exposed; an unseemly spectacle, and the degrading memorial of popular frenzy.

The walls, which had withstood the lawless fury of a mob, were destined to fall by the unskilfulness of an architect. The roof of the church being ruinous, Duke Hamilton, heritable keeper of the palace, represented its condition to the Barons of Exchequer, praying that it might be repaired,

An architect and a mason were accordingly consulted. Their united wisdom soon displayed itself. The walls of the church were already six hundred years old, and might be presumed to be in no very firm condition: yet this architect and mason proposed to put on them a roof of flag stones, instead of one composed of slate. Their suggestion was adopted, and their estimate of the expense approved by the Barons of Exchequer, 7th August, 1758. The new roof very soon injured the fabric. A report was made to the Barons by another architect, of somewhat more judgment, who predicted that the church would very soon become ruinous if the massy roof, which the walls were never constructed to support, was not removed. He had the fate of Cassandra. His prophecy was neglected: but it was soon fulfilled, for on the 2d December, 1768, the church fell.

Popular rapacity and sacrilege were again active. What had escaped the ravages of the mob at the revolution now became their property. The church was ransacked, and every thing stolen that could be converted into money. The bones of the dead were even removed, though some were suffered to remain an indecent and mortifying spectacle. The head of Queen Margaret, which was entire, and even beautiful, and the skull of Darnley, were purloined. Of Darnley! the haughty, the imperious, but the fascinating lover of the unfortunate Mary! How aptly might its possessors have moralized upon this relic in the words of Shakspeare:

" Now get you to my lady's chamber, and tell her, let her paint an inch thick, to this favour she must come; make her laugh at that."

The thigh bones of this ambitious noble were left, and their extraordinary magnitude fully proved all that historians relate of the vastness of his stature.* Could he have had one foreboding thought when he was high in hope and mighty in power, when he beheld the multitude gazing at that form with feelings of mingled awe and admiration, that in after-times his mouldering bones would be torn from their sepulchre, exhibited to the idle gaze of vulgar curiosity, or tossed aside with rude indifference, what a

---

* It is said he was seven feet in height.

humiliating reproof must have touched his heart, even in the very plenitude of that dominion he so fondly coveted and so amply enjoyed!

It may be added, in conclusion, that there are in the belfry a marble monument and statue of Robert Lord Bellhaven, who died in 1639. The figure is reclining at full length, and the execution is masterly, but somewhat mutilated by the falling in of the roof. Of this Lord Bellhaven Burnet relates the following anecdote, in his History of his own Times. Charles I. in the third year of his reign, sent the Earl of Nithsdale into Scotland, with a power to take the surrender of all church lands, and to assure those who readily surrendered, that the king would take it kindly and use them well, but that he would proceed with all rigour against those who would not submit their rights to his disposal.

"Upon his coming down," continues Burnet, "those who were most concerned in such grants met at Edinburgh, and agreed, that when they were called together, if no other argument did prevail to make the Earl of Nithsdale desist, they would fall upon him and all his party in the old Scottish manner, and knock them on the head. Primrose told me one of these lords, Bellhaven, of the name of Douglas, who was blind, bid them sit him by one of the party, and he would make sure of one. So he was set next to the Earl of Dumfries: he was all the while holding him fast; and when the other asked him what he meant by that? he said, Ever since the blindness was come on him he was in such fear of falling, that he could not help holding fast to those who were next to him. He had, all the while, a poniard in his other hand, with which he had certainly stabbed Dumfries if any disorder had happened."

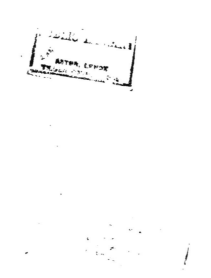

NAWORTH CASTLE,
Cumberland

Engraved for Grays Views & Drawings by I. Cheesell, to the Border Antiquities of England and Scotland

𝔑𝔞𝔴𝔬𝔯𝔱𝔥 𝔠𝔞𝔰𝔱𝔩𝔢,

CUMBERLAND.

THIS gothic edifice was, in former times, one of those extensive baronial seats which marked the splendor of our ancient nobles, before they exchanged the hospitable magnificence of a life spent among a numerous tenantry, for the uncertain honours of court attendance, and the equivocal rewards of ministerial favour. If we allow that the feudal times were times of personal insecurity, we must also admit that they were favourable to the growth of manly and decided virtue; rude and unpolished in its structure, perhaps, but forcible and efficient in its operation. The evils of the institution were in some measure corrected by other qualities inherent in its system, while the good was pure and unmixed. There is a principle of affinity, more or less obvious, in every thing. The vast and solid mansions of our ancient nobility were like their characters; greatness without elegance, strength without refinement; but lofty, firm, and commanding.

The solemn grandeur of Naworth Castle, claimed for it a high distinction among these baronial edifices; and, as it is still entire, a more exact account of it may be given than can always be obtained. It once belonged, according to Pennant, to the Dacres, but became afterwards by marriage the property of William Lord Howard, commonly known by the name of *Bauld Willey*.

The whole arrangement of the buildings forms a square; but we have no certain information as to the period of its erection. In the south side is a gateway, with the arms of the Dacres; over the door, those of the Howards. Tradition says this castle was built by the Dacres, but by which of them is not ascertained. One of them, Robert de Dacre, from a quotation in Madox's History of the Exchequer, seems to have been sheriff in Cumberland 39 Hen. III.; and another, Ranulph de Dacre, 14th Edw. I. constable

M

of the Tower.   The first mention of this castle is in the reign of Edward II. when, in the 18th of that reign, it appears from Madox's Baronia, that William de Dacre, son and heir of Hugh de Dacre, who was brother and heir of Ranulph de Dacre, held it, with the manor of Irchington, to which it belonged; also the manors of Burgh, near Sands, Lasingby and Farlham, and other lands, by the service of one entire barony, and of doing homage and fealty to the king, and of yielding to him for cornage, at his exchequer at Carlisle, yearly, at the feast of the Assumption of St. Mary, 51s. 8d. It continued in the family of the Dacres till the year 1569, when, on the 17th May, according to Stowe, " George Lord Dacre, of Graystoke, sonne and heire of Thomas Lord Dacre, being a child in yeeres, and then ward to Thomas Lord Howard, Duke of Norfolk, was by a great mischaunce slaine at Thetford, in the house of Sir Richard Falmenstone, Knight, by meane of a vauting horse of wood standing within the same house; upon which horse as he meant to have vauted, and the pinnes at the feet being not made sure, the horse fell upon him, and bruised the brains out of his head."

In the January following, Leonard Dacre, Esq. of Horsly, in the county of York, second son to Lord William Dacre of Gilsland, " choosing," according to Camden, " rather to try for the estate with his prince in war than with his nieces at law," entered into a rebellion, with design to carry off the Queen of Scots: but being disappointed by her removal to Coventry, and having the command of three thousand men, which he had been entrusted to raise for the Queen's service, he seized several castles, among which were those of Graystock and Naworth; but being attacked and defeated by Lord Hunsdon,* at the head of the garrison of Berwick, he fled to Flanders, where he died.

* He was the father of Sir Robert Cary, Earl of Monmouth. In Sir Robert Naunton's Fragmenta Regalia there is a well drawn character of this nobleman. " He was a fast man," says he, " to his prince, and firm in his friends and servants, and though he might speak big, and therein would be borne out, yet was he not the more dreadful, but less harmful, and far from the practice of my Lord of Leicester's instructions, for he was downright: and I have heard those that both knew him well, and had interest in him, say merrily of him, that his Latin and his

The castle next came into the possession of Lord William Howard, the third son of Thomas Duke of Norfolk, in right of his wife Elizabeth, sister of George the last Lord Dacre, before mentioned. In 1607, when Camden visited it, it was under repair; and Bishop Gibson says it was again repaired and made fit for the reception of a family by the Right Honourable Charles Howard, great grandson to the preceding Lord William. It is now the seat of the Earl of Carlisle; but is seldom occupied, we believe.

The approach to this gothic structure is striking and picturesque. The front is strengthened by a curtain wall and a gateway embrazured, and the corners of the chief building on this side by lofty square towers. On the north it impends over the river Irthing, at a great height: the banks shagged with wood. "The whole house," says Pennant, "is a true specimen of ancient inconvenience, of magnificence and littleness; the rooms numerous, accessible by sixteen staircases, with most frequent and sudden ascents and descents into the bargain." The entrance into the hall strikes the traveller with all the solemn magnificence of antiquity. This apartment is seventy-eight feet in length, very lofty, and of a proportionable width. The ceiling is formed of wood pannels, in large squares; and the upper end of the hall is wainscotted in the same manner. The pannels are in number one hundred and twenty-nine,* on which are painted portraits of

dissimulation were both alike, and that his custom of swearing and obscenity in speaking made him seem a worse Christian than he was, and a better knight of the carpet than he should be: as he lived in a ruffling time, so he loved sword and buckler men, and such as our fathers were wont to call men of their hands, of which sort he had many brave gentlemen that followed him; yet not taken for a popular and dangerous person: and that is one that stood amongst the Togati, of an honest stout heart, and such a one as, upon occasion, would have fought for his prince and country: for he had the charge of the queen's person, both in the court and in the camp at Tilbury."

See also, in the *Memoirs of Sir Robert Cary*, his son, a curious letter from him to Lord Treasurer Burleigh, requesting the loan of 1000*l.* to enable him to go down and assume his command at Berwick.

* This is Mr. Hutchinson's account: Hist. of Cumb. vol. i. 134. Pennant says, there are only 107 squares. See Grose, Antiq. of England and Wales, vol. i. p. 56.

the Saxon kings, and the sovereigns of England, down to the union of the houses of York and Lancaster, with many noble personages: they have, however, no other recommendation but their antiquity. " They were brought," according to a person who visited the castle in 1732 (vide Grose) " from Kirkoswald castle when that was demolished." At the bottom of the hall is a gallery of modern work, which, it is presumed, fills the place of one of greater antiquity. In ancient times it was the custom on festival days to entertain the guests in these galleries with music, shows, and masques: it is now adorned with four vast crests carved in wood, viz. a griffin and dolphin, with the scallops; a unicorn, and an ox with a coronet round his neck. In front is a figure in wood of an armed man; two others, perhaps vassals, in short jackets and caps; a pouch pendant behind, and the mutilated remains of a priapus to each: one has wooden shoes. These seem to have been the *Ludibrium Aulæ* in those gross days. The chimney-piece here is five yards and a half broad. Within this is another apartment, hung with old tapestry; a head of Anne of Cleves and several family portraits remain there. The whole castle bears the strongest memorials of ancient customs, and the inconvenient modes of domestic life which our ancestors adopted. The old windows are narrow and grated, and the doors almost wholly cased with iron, moving on ponderous hinges, and with massive bolts which make a harsh and horrid clang, that echoes fearfully through the winding passages. The mouldings of several of the apartments are gilt or painted, the ceilings figured, the mantle-pieces sculptured with coat armour, and the chambers hung with gloomy tapestry.

The chapel is below stairs, and formed in a very antique style, with a pulpit and stall of oak; at the end, opposite the altar, are closets for the superiors of the family attending divine service. The ceiling and altar end is wainscoted in pannels like the hall, painted with portraits of the patriarchs, several of the kings of Israel and Judah, and others: in all 58. A long elevated stall faces the pulpit, which perhaps was the place of the chief domestics; above it are blazoned all the arms of the Howards, from Fulcho to 1623 and 1644, with the families with whom they had made alliances, or from whom they were descended; under the shields of arms

the name of each personage is placed. " Under a great sprawling figure
of an old man," says Grose, " with a branch rising from him on the ceiling
is written Pictor * MDXII. On the great window, in glass, are represented
a knight and a lady kneeling ; on their mantles pictured these arms, three
escallops and checquers."

In the garden walls were stones with Roman inscriptions, collected probably from the Picts' wall : a general account of these stones is given in
Horsley's Britannia Romana. Camden, who also mentions them, has
copied some of the inscriptions. They are now removed. ,

The apartments of Lord William Howard remain to be described. He
was the terror of the moss troopers, and though he ruled the country with
military rigour, yet he produced much good among a race of inhabitants as
barbarous and uncultivated as ever possessed a settlement in this island.
He kept constantly 140 men here as his guard. The approach to his
apartments was secured by plated doors, several in succession, fastened by
immense locks and bolts of iron, defending a narrow winding staircase
where only one person could pass at a time. The ceiling is figured, and the
mantle-piece has the arms and motto of the Howards. There is a narrow
gallery, 140 feet in length, which led to sundry apartments ; and among
others to the library, which is stored with a great number of ancient books :
it is in a very secret place near the top of one of the towers. " Not a book
has been added since his days, i. e. since those of Queen Elizabeth," according to Pennant ; but Hutchinson says this is erroneous. In the library
is a vast case, three feet high, which opens into three leaves, having six
great pages pasted on it, being an account of St Joseph of Aramathea and
his twelve disciples, who founded Glastonbury: and, at the end, a long
history of saints, with the number of years or days for which each could
grant indulgences. The roof is carved, but not with much elegance : the
windows are high, and can be ascended only by three stone steps : such
was the caution of the times. It is reported that Lord William was very

* " Magister Lucas Egliment Pictor," according to Hutchinson.

studious, and wrote much. The following anecdote proves not only his love of study, but the implicit alacrity with which his orders were obeyed.

Once, when he was thus employed with his books, a servant came to tell him that a prisoner had been just brought in, and desired to know what should be done with him. " Hang him !" exclaimed Lord William peevishly, and resumed the subject of his meditation. When he had finished what he was about, he recollected the prisoner, and ordered that he should be brought before him for examination; but he found that his heedless expression had been construed into a command, and the unfortunate captive had been immediately hung up. A potent noble in those days was a petty prince ; and the bitter reflection which Shakespeare puts into the mouth of King John, upon hearing of Arthur's death, might have aptly occurred to Lord William.

> It is the curse of kings, to be attended
> By slaves, that take their humours for a warrant,
> To break within the bloody house of life :
> And, on the winking of authority,
> To understand a law; to know the meaning
> Of dangerous majesty, when, perchance, it frowns
> More upon humour than advised respect.

The dungeon of this castle instils horror into the beholder ; consisting of four dark apartments, three below, and one above, up a long staircase, all well secured : in the uppermost, one ring remains, to which criminals were chained, and the marks remain of many more such fastening places. Miserable abodes ! where the wretched captive lingered out a hopeless life, shut from the sweet varieties of nature, the converse of friend or relative, and all that renders existence valuable by giving us an interest in its preservation.

Near the library is the oratory or private chapel, well secured, where Lord William enjoyed his religion in privacy. The ceiling and walls are richly ornamented with coats of arms and carvings in wood, painted and gilt. On one side is a good painting on wood, in the style of Lucas Van

Leyden, representing the flagellation of our Saviour, his crucifixion, and resurrection. Here also is a fine piece of sculpture in alto-relievo, in marble, of the crucifixion : some tolerable pieces of the like work, representing our Saviour saluted by Judas; the Descent of the Holy Spirit; an abbess with a sword in her hand, attending a crowned personage falling on his sword; a monk with a crowned head in his hand, and several others of considerable value. Many of them were probably saved from the monastery at the dissolution.

Lord William Howard is frequently the hero of Border minstrelsy, under the appellation of *Belted Will Howard*, or *Belted Willie*. Walter Scott, in his Lay of the Last Minstrel, conducts William of Deloraine to Naworth castle, where he is supposed to have been imprisoned three months, till he paid a ransom of a thousand marks. Belted Will is said, in general, to have been just, though seldom merciful. The place of execution was a grove of aged oak-trees near the castle, on which many a Border marauder, both Scottish and English, struggled his last. The present noble proprietor, (the Earl of Carlisle) deserves high praise for the attention bestowed in maintaining this curious and venerable pile in its ancient state; and we cannot better conclude this account of Naworth castle than with the following descriptive lines from the pen of its noble owner.

O Naworth! monument of rudest times,
When science slept entombed, and o'er the waste,
The heath grown crag, and quivering moss, of old
Stalked unremitted war! The call for blood
A herd purloined, perchance a ravaged flock;
For this how often have thy dungeons, caves
Of sad despair, been fed with those, whose hands,
More fit to wield the scythe or spade, upreared
The enormous pike! while all in iron clad,
As plunder tempted or their chieftain led,
Joined the fierce rout of predatory force,
Making our Border tremble. Ah! how oft
These oaks, that fling their leafless arms so high,
And warn the traveller, erring from his way,
(Best office of their age) have pitying heard

The veteran's dying groan; beheld him dragged
To an unworthy death, and marked the voice,
That to a long descent, and distant time,
Left the dire legacy of deep revenge.
If on yon mountain's slippery ridge, where once,
From man's annoyance safe, the wild stag broused,
Lord of this heathy world; and where the eagle
Defied the invader of his rocky bed:
Now the plantation, gay with different tints,
Drives its new shadow o'er the wond'ring lake;
If now the waving corn has dared to hide,
Within its yellow breast the proud remains
Of Roman toils, magnificence, and power;
If now the peasant, scared no more at eve
By distant beacons, and compelled to house
His trembling flocks, his children and his all,
Beneath his craggy roof, securely sleeps;
Yet all around thee is not changed: thy towers,
Unmodernized by tasteless art, remain
Still unsubdued by time.

PART OF

WIDDRINGTON CASTLE.

Northumberland

Prudhoe Castle,

PRUDHOE or Prudhow castle, is pleasantly situated on the summit of a vast rocky promontory on the south side of and near the river Tyne, eight miles west of Newcastle. It was formerly the baronial residence of the ancient family of the Umfranvilles, and afterwards for many years one of the castles of the Percies. Camden supposes that this place was the Protolitia or Procolitia of the Romans, which was the station of the first cohort of the Batavi. With this barony Robert de Umfranville was infeoffed by king Henry I., who gave him the royal privileges and franchises of Reeds-dale, and the castles of Otterburn and Harbottle. The castle of Prudhoe he held by the service of two knights fees and a half;* and Reeds-dale by that of defending it from thieves and wolves: two names for the same character.

In the reign of Henry II. 1174, Odonel de Humfranville was owner of this castle when it was besieged, but in vain, by William king of Scots. Sir William Dugdale says, in his Baronage, according to the monk of Tinemouth, in the 18th of Henry II., " This Odonel greatly oppressed and plundered his neighbours, in order to repair the roof of his castle at Prudhow, presuming on his own eminence and the interest he was possessed of by having married his daughter to one high in the king's favour." He held this castle till his death, which happened in the 28th of Henry II. He was succeeded by Robert his son, whose successor Richard delivered up his four sons

---

* The general reader, not acquainted with the peculiarities of feudal service, may require to be informed that a portion of land, of which the grant, by the agreement of the giver and receiver, entitled to the service of a soldier or a knight, was a *knight's fee*. An estate of two hundred fees furnished, of consequence, two hundred knights. But these knights of tenure must not be confounded with the knight of honour, a creation of a higher order in the scale of chivalry, and bestowed only for eminent prowess or distinguished virtues.

N

and his castle of Prudhoe to king John as pledges of his fidelity. These securities, however, did not prevent him from joining with the barons in that holy war of patriotism which they waged against the fickle tyrant, and in consequence his castle and lands were given to Hugh de Baliol. In the succeeding reign, however, he obtained a restitution of them. He died 11th Henry III., having given one toft and eight acres of land in the town of Prudhoe to the monks of Hexham. His son Gilbert succeeded to his barony, who is styled by our historians " the famous baron, the flower and keeper of the northern parts of England." To him succeeded a son of the same name (1245), who founded a chantry in the chapel of our Lady, at his castle of Prudhoe, and endowed it with two tofts and 118 acres of land, and five acres of meadow, for the maintenance of two chaplains to perform divine service daily therein. He was created Earl of Angus in Scotland by Edward I., and under that title summoned to the Parliament in 1297. The castle and its appendages continued in the family till it passed into that of the Percies by marriage, about the year 1381, since which period it has constituted a part of the princely possessions of the Duke of Northumberland, with only such interruptions as were occasioned by attainders in different periods.

The present condition of this mansion remains to be described. It is guarded by an outward wall towards the Tyne, built on the brink of the cliffs, in this place not less than sixty perpendicular feet in height, above the plain which intervenes between the castle and the river. This wall, at intervals, is defended by square bastions. The entrance to the castle is from the south: when viewed from the heights, the whole structure has a very noble and formidable appearance. Mr. Hutchinson, who seems to have examined very minutely the actual state of this mansion, has given the following description of it. " The narrow neck of land," says he, " leading to the entrance, was formerly cut through by a deep ditch, over which a drawbridge has given access to the outward gate: the water which anciently supplied the ditch is now collected by a reservoir before the gate, and serves a mill: the outward gate was originally defended by several outworks and a tower, as appears by their ruins. From the situa-

tion in which I drew my view of this place, I could overlook the top of the first gate, and the eye penetrated the inner gateway; the superstructure of which is a lofty embattled square tower, about sixty feet high, now so mantled with ivy that the windows, loop-holes, and apertures, are almost wholly concealed. To the right the outward wall extended to some distance, terminated by a turret or exploratory mount, the wall of which is embattled, and there the landscape was closed by a fine grove of stately trees. The outward wall to the left, from the inner gateway, extends to a considerable distance without any turret or bastion, over which several interior buildings, and among them the remains of the chapel, were discovered in all the confusion of ruin : mingled chimneys, windows, buttresses, columns, and walls, in that wildness of irregularity which constitutes much picturesque beauty in scenes of this kind ; above all which objects, a square tower, the keep of the fortress (on the side towards me almost perfect, twenty-five yards in height and eighteen in breadth, but without ornament or windows, with an exploratory tower on the south-west corner), overlooked the castle with that gloomy and sullen majesty which characterizes the age in which it had its rise. The wall still extending to the left, on its angle is defended by a square bastion, with broken loop-holes, from whence it turns northward, and is terminated by a broken circular tower, situate on the brink of the cliff, whose inner recess the eye sufficiently penetrated to mark the distraction of its interior works. The fine levels between the castle and the river, opened to the left, the Tyne in view, with the town of Ovingham hanging on the opposite shore.

" We advanced by a narrow path on the side of the reservoir to the first gateway, which is formed by a circular arch : by the fragments and broken walls it evidently appears this gate was originally flanked with various outworks and had a tower. This gate gives admittance to a covered way, leading to the inner gate, about 30 paces in length; a sallyport opening on each side, to flank the walls and defend the ditch. There is no appearance of a portcullis in either gateway. The second gateway is also formed by a circular arch, above which is a high tower, the windows shewing that it contained three tiers of apartments. A lattice or open gate still remains, jointed with studs of iron. The roof of the gateway is arched in semicircles, with an aperture in the centre, from whence those in the upper chamber might annoy an enemy who had forced the gate. From thence you enter an area, now so blocked up by the buildings of a farm-yard and tenement, that it is not possible to form any idea of its original magnitude: though it appears by the other part that an open area had surrounded the great tower, which doth not shew any remains of communication with the outworks, but seems to have stood apart on an eminence in the centre. The outward wall was defended on the angle to the south-west by a large square bastion with loop-holes; to the north-west by a circular tower, containing several tiers of low chambers, singular in their form and height, and such as I never observed before in any ancient castle: the inhabitants could not stand erect in them at the time of defence. Towards the river and northward the wall is guarded by several small square bastions; and towards the south-east, a small mount, placed within the walls, overlooks the ditch which guards the southern side, and terminates at the brink of the cliffs. The large tower is in ruins, only the southern wall now standing, and not one bastion remains entire, they being all in ruins towards the area. A passage runs in the centre of the wall from bastion to bastion. Steps ascend from the area to the top of the walls in several places, which is broad enough to allow the armed men of the garrison to pass each other, covered by a rampart."

In the fourth volume of Grose's Antiquities of England, p. 137, there is a description of this castle from an old survey taken in 1586, and which that ingenious antiquary was permitted to copy from the archives of the Northumberland family. It affords some points of curious comparison with the present appearance of the building.

Lightning Source UK Ltd.
Milton Keynes UK
UKOW04f152290716

279521UK00001B/99/P